Peter Pan and Cricket

PETER PAN
& CRICKET

David Rayvern Allen

CONSTABLE · LONDON

First published in Great Britain 1988
by Constable and Company Limited
10 Orange Street London WC2H 7EG
Copyright © 1988 David Rayvern Allen
Set in Linotron Plantin by
Rowland Phototypesetting Limited
Bury St Edmunds, Suffolk
Printed in Great Britain by
St Edmundsbury Press Limited
Bury St Edmunds, Suffolk

British Library CIP data

Allen, David Rayvern
Peter Pan and cricket
1. Barrie, J. M. – Biography   2. Authors,
Scottish – 19th century – Biography
3. Authors, Scottish – 20th century –
Biography
I. Title
822'.8   PR4076

ISBN 0 09 467630 5

'Cricket is an idea. It was an idea of the Gods'

CONTENTS

CONTENTS

ILLUSTRATIONS

[9]

ACKNOWLEDGEMENTS

There are many who help on the way to making a book. For this particular one, two ladies were of immeasurable assistance. Elizabeth Drainer and Karen Gilmour care devotedly for the fascinating relics within Barrie's birthplace at Kirriemuir and from there they dispense warmth, sustenance and an unforgettable enthusiasm for the subject which is wholly contagious.

Likewise, Andrew Birkin, whose memorable appraisal of *J. M. Barrie and the Lost Boys* is surely the definitive study of that relationship, was unreservedly kind and generous with information and help.

My grateful thanks also to the following who all made contributions that were never less than entirely supportive and in many cases much more: Peter Adamson, staff at the BBC Reference Library, the British Library at Bloomsbury and the Colindale Newspaper Division, Hal Cohen, the late Jim Coldham, Dorothea Edwards, David Frith, Benny Green, Stephen Green, Bunty Ireland, Tim Jollands, Tony Laughton, Alan Mackay, John McKenzie, the Viola Meynell collection, the National Portrait Gallery of Scotland, John Pawsey, Gaston Phillips, Richard Streeton, Shane Togher, Richard Tomkins and Tony Winder. Appreciation is due, as well, to an understanding wife who helped compile the Index.

Barrie assigned royalties from productions of *Peter Pan* to the Hospital for Sick Children at Great Ormond Street in London. Although the copyright period for that indelible creation has run its course, a proportion of the royalties accrued from this book will be channelled to the same place, where so many in desperate need find help and hope.

For the illustrations I am indebted to: Peter Adamson, Andrew Birkin, Dr J. G. Burgess, David Frith, Stephen Green and Tony Laughton.

1

KIRRIEMUIR TO SLOWCUM PODGER AND BACK

T HE biographical bones of J. M. Barrie have been turned over with great frequency by those who, bewitched in childhood by the creations of his febrile imagination, have wondered ever after where on earth he found his Never-Never Land. The fascination that Barrie has held over generation upon generation of semi-literate children and adults, both literary in taste and otherwise, since the day in 1904 when Nina Boucicault as Peter Pan asked: 'Do you believe in fairies?', has been matched only by his own penchant for possessing people on whom to cast his spell. J. A. Hammerton, W. A. Darlington and Denis Mackail are but three luminaries who stand out from the throng of Barrie-querists who have tried to trace where fact ended and fantasy began. Up to now, all the books on Barrie and his writings have, naturally enough, concentrated on the events of his life, his novels and plays and, fundamentally, psychological interpretations of his often strange behaviour. Barrie's great affection for cricket has sometimes been part of their story but always incidental to the main theme. In this modest volume, we will attempt to make his preoccupation with the game the main theme and everything else incidental.

In his study of Barrie, F. J. Harvey Darton found 'the elements so mixed'.

In the spacious days of cricket there used often to be seen in the vast wilderness of the Mound Stand at Lord's a small lonely figure smoking a pipe. Aloof and solitary, he gazed in a sombre rapture at the white moving shapes, so steadily that he seemed to be a fixture, like the clock or the pavilion. You would not have thought that he was a Scot, for Caledonia is almost too stern and wild for cricket; that he might have, at that very moment, two or three plays running in

London, and the 'best-seller' of the year being clamoured for at the circulating libraries; that he was a Doctor of Laws of one great Scottish University, Rector of another, a member of the Order of Merit, and a baronet of the United Kingdom. But so it was. Sir James Matthew Barrie was, if not a cricket fan, at least a devotee . . . the game has always been a passion with him, and love of it is certainly one of the things that has made Barrie what he is – whatever that may be . . .

How was it, then, that a very Scotty Scot, 'part mother, part hero-worshipping maiden, part grandfather and part pixie with no man in him at all' – to use a description by Desmond McCarthy – came to have a lifelong love affair with cricket? As in much to do with Barrie, there are superficially easy answers as well as answers of mind-bewildering complexity. Infuriatingly, they could all be right and readers are conveniently invited to make their own concentric circles, and perhaps conclusions, from the pages that follow.

We should remember that the laddie from Thrums (born in 1860) grew up in a Forfarshire where cricket of no mean standard was being played. In assessments of the game in Britain during the last century, Scotland nearly always gets overlooked, but there were several fine players and much good cricket and not only in the military centres or from expatriate Englishmen. Brechin could undoubtedly claim to be one of the oldest clubs north of the border and had regular fixtures against Kirriemuir. Some of the matches were played on the 'Hill' above Barrie's birthplace and he spent many happy hours watching, scoring and noting, often in the company of his elder brother who was a keen follower of averages. At other times, Barrie amused himself with extemporary games on Kirrie Hill, played with a home-made bat and a flat boulder as a wicket, wearing his jacket inside out as a sign that he was a member of the 'club'.

One of the Brechin side was the all-rounder Dundas, who 'was acknowledged to be the greatest player in the County in the seventies'. Apart from being a hard-hitting striker, Dundas had performed several phenomenal feats with the ball since his return from regimental service abroad. Alfred O'Neill's *Annals of Brechin Cricket* reveals all. 'In 1871, playing against Montrose at Montrose he did the "hat-trick", and when batting drove four successive balls for six runs each. Every run had then to be run out. In the return game at Brechin that same year he had 58 not out to his credit, while in the first innings of Montrose he again did the "hat-trick", and in the

[14]

second "went two better" by dismissing five of their players with successive balls.' Notably though, 'against Kirriemuir the same season he took four wickets with successive balls. When he left [Brechin] for Kirriemuir he raised the standard of the club there, and made many large scores.' It is perhaps pertinent to remember that J. A. Hammerton, writing nearly sixty years after these events, noted that 'the game has always been in high favour at Kirriemuir, and even now is not outdone by football'.

Later, Dundas left Kirriemuir to play for a Forfar club and it would be interesting to know what the young J.M.B. managed to glean, in between his academic studies at, successively, Glasgow, Forfar and Dumfries, when watching him bowling his 'wily underhand' lobs on the rough and uneven pitches of the day.

Once 'Jamie' Barrie had reached Dumfries Academy, in the autumn of 1873, he felt a great sense of anticipation. The fact that the school was recognized as one of the twelve best in Scotland, whose educational standards were far ahead of those in England at that time, meant little to him. Of more importance was the realization that cricket and football were played there and that next summer he would be able to turn out with a proper bat and bowl at real stumps. A proper bat to Barrie was one with a cane handle, that did not jar the hands when striking the ball – and one's mind leaps unsequentially to the line in 'Old Hyphen' where 'Ma kicked Mi for bursting a cane-handled bat while digging for worms with it'.

During the winter months at the Academy the fledgeling sportsman enjoyed donning football boots and kicking a ball about, though he gave as much time to marbles, at which he displayed a ferocious aptitude, to the extent of wearing out the sole of his boot which he scraped along the ground in the act of delivery. Nothing, however, could displace cricket in his affections and it was whilst wandering around the perimeter of the field after an inter-school game and watching, from a distance, the victors and vanquished toast themselves in treacle beer that Barrie had the notion of writing reports on these matches for the local papers. He had, about that time, been induced to offer the four-part 'Reckolections of a Schoolmaster (misspelling in the style of Jack Billings)' and some verses on The Seven Ages of Man for the school magazine, *The Clown*, so not unnaturally thoughts on the power of the pen were in his mind. Not that there was any comparison between manuscript contributions in-house and the printed page for public consumption, albeit that brief write-ups of sporting activities in the press tended to appear anonymously. Therefore, looking through the games reports in the *Dumfries and Galloway Standard and Advertiser* over a century later, it is virtually impossible to be certain of

[15]

Barrie's hand. He had himself taken part in a number of the Academy matches, first appearing for the school in 1875 batting at number eleven and then, in the ensuing years, being promoted up the order to number three.

It was as a bowler, however, that he achieved noteworthy figures. In a game against Hutton Hall Academy in June 1877, Barrie mopped up the tail with four wickets. The *Dumfries and Galloway Standard and Advertiser* gave the details:

FIRST ELEVEN DUMFRIES ACADEMY V. FIRST ELEVEN HUTTON HALL

A match between these clubs was played on the ground of the latter on Saturday; and they succeeded in obtaining an easy victory over their antagonists by 72 runs. Dickson and Fidler did capital service for the home team, the former retiring for a good score of 24; the latter completely baffled all efforts of his eager opponents by his magnificent batting, in which he displayed some scientific cuts and drives, and succeeded in carrying out his bat for a splendid score of 53 runs, a feat which is seldom attained by juvenile cricketers. The strangers were not able to withstand the excellent bowling of Rennie and Dickson, and were soon disposed of – Johnstone and Thomson being the only two who obtained a score. The following is the result:

HUTTON HALL ACADEMY

W. Bell, c Newbigging, b Hogg	3
W. Sloan, b Hogg	4
J. King, b Hogg	3
J. Rennie, b Thomson	5
A. Dickson, c and b Thomson	24
M. Little, b Thomson	2
J. G. Fiddler, not out	53
W. Ellis, st Thomson, b Barrie	0
J. Crook, b Barrie	7
W. Sherwen, c and b Barrie	2
R. Mitchell, c Thomson, b Barrie	6
Extras	12
	121

DUMFRIES ACADEMY

J. Hogg, b Rennie	5
H. McEwen, b Rennie	0
J. Barrie, b Dickson	1
J. Callander, b Rennie	5
G. Thomson, st Little, b Rennie	9
W. Foster, b Dickson	0
C. Wilson, b Dickson	0
W. Johnston, st Little, b Rennie	13
J. Newbigging, c Sherwen, b Dickson	2
R. Paton, b Rennie	3
J. Richardson, not out	1
Extras	10
	49

The town of Dumfries also had the distinction of seeing Barrie's first dramatic effort, mounted at the Assembly Rooms in the winter of 1876: *Le petit drame sensationel, en six tableaux – Bandelero the Bandit.* Barrie himself appeared as a character called Smike and was delighted when the play was denounced by a local minister who thought it grossly immoral; the ensuing furore which reached the columns of the London papers made the young playwright something of a celebrity at his school.

After leaving the Academy in 1878, Barrie went to Edinburgh University and spent four years in the city experiencing, no doubt, its 'snell, blae, nirly and scowthering' winds – a description of Robert Louis Stevenson's – and the ichor in its air which if it did not stir his blood perhaps excited his imagination. Almost certainly a flight of fancy as well as the passage of time helped the authenticity of Barrie's recollection when, in a speech in 1926, he told of literally bumping into R. L. Stevenson in Princes Street:

He passed on, but he had bumped against me, and I stood in the middle of the street, regardless of the traffic, and glared contemptuously after him. He must have grown conscious of this, because he turned around and looked at me. I continued to glare. He went on a little bit, and turned around again. I was still glaring, and he came back and said to me, quite nicely: 'After all, God made me.' I said:

[17]

'He is getting careless.' He lifted his cane, and then, instead, he said: 'Do I know you?' He said it with such extraordinary charm that I replied, wistfully: 'No, but I wish you did.' He said: 'Let's pretend I do,' and we went off to a tavern at the foot of Leith Street, where we drank what he said was the favourite wine of the Three Musketeers. Each of us wanted to pay, but it did not much matter, as neither of us had any money.

Stevenson's and Barrie's time in Edinburgh overlapped by nearly a year so it would be churlish to dispute such a romantic encounter, especially as in later years Barrie quoted a letter from Stevenson in which he said that two who had used the dreadful lavatory at Edinburgh University, though they never met, could never quite be strangers. Be that as it may, however, inevitably the young student came into contact with a number of distinguished men of letters. Among them was his own professor, David Masson, and also John Stuart Blackie. They were two of *An Edinburgh Eleven*, a series of character sketches penned under Barrie's pseudonym, Gavin Ogilvy, which appeared originally in the *British Weekly* from 1887 before eventually finding book form. The other nine comprised Lord Rosebery, Professors Calderwood, Tait, Fraser, Chrystal and Sellar, Joseph Thomson, the explorer, the aforementioned R. L. Stevenson and The Revd W. C. Smith DD. It was the author, Sir Arthur Quiller-Couch, often to be found in items of Barriana simply monogrammed 'Q', who reminded readers in his *Speaker* (he was then assistant editor) that when J.M.B. put together eleven men of name and fame in and beyond the Scottish capital he called them *An Edinburgh Eleven* for the same reason that 'fond admirers speak of Mr Arthur Shrewsbury (upon whose renown it is notorious that the sun never sets) as "the Notts Professional", and of a yet more illustrious cricketer by his paltry title of "Doctor" –

> Not so much honouring thee,
> As giving it a hope that there
> It could not withered be.'

Therefore, *An Edinburgh Eleven* is obviously a convenient cricket-lover's title though not a cricketer's book. Barrie, writing to Robertson Nicoll, editor of the *British Weekly* in 1921, recalled how even the high and mighty were fooled: 'Do you remember how, early in the life of the *British Weekly*, I wrote some papers for you on Scottish worthies, which were afterwards

[18]

published as a little volume under the title "An Edinburgh Eleven"? And how Dr W. G. Grace came across it and tossed it aside on discovering that not one of my eleven could bat or bowl?'

Barrie's perambulations had so far been limited. Now, having been 'capped and balled' an MA, in April 1882, he experienced an unsettling period in limbo, knowing that he wanted to write, but not knowing where to write. Eventually, his sister, Jane Ann, saw an advertisement in the pages of *The Scotsman* for a leader writer on the *Nottingham Journal* at a salary of £3 a week. Barrie applied, got the job and headed south. For the next twenty months, during 1883 and 1884, he became 'Hippomenes' (Atalanta's ingenious but unsportsmanlike opponent) on Mondays and 'A Modern Peripatetic' on Thursdays: both articles under these signatures were then reprinted in the Weekly Supplement. This, together with an average of twelve hundred words a day as leader writer and the added toil of book reviews made sure that he had consistent practice and was under constant pressure. The *Journal* had no editor as such, the final directing hand seemed to be that of the foreman compositor in the early hours of each morning, therefore the learner-journalist had an almost totally free hand in his choice of subjects. Barrie had always been adept at making topics of potentially stultifying boredom come alive on the page – 'I was once challenged to write an article about a scrap of paper that had been blown into the gutter, and I found it quite easy'; now, in a provincial conurbation that was little more than a string of villages looped together, his ingenuity was stretched to capacity. Mind you, cricket of any kind could never, of course, be classified in any other category than as totally fascinating. Barrie seized the opportunity:

A RURAL CRICKET MATCH

The cricketers of Slowcum Podger do not own a professional, and, of course, for the very simple reason that they do not require one. Could a professional bowl twisters such as those with which old Christopher Sly in his best days used to take an average of two wickets an over? True Christopher passed his best days long ago, and no one remembers his former feats nearly so vividly as himself, but what of that. Christopher would scorn to tell a lie, and cricket, like angling, makes a man very circumspect about what he says. You can as implicitly believe the cricketer who tells a story of how he (in the old days again)

[19]

never ran for anything less than a four, as you can trust the angler when he swears that had it not been for the treacherous state of the bank he would have landed a salmon weighing forty-two pounds and a half. Now, at Lord's, for instance, one never hears a professional or a 'gentleman' boasting of his former deeds, which at once proves that he has none to boast of. But as it is unprofitable labour to try to kill a dead sheep, it is not here necessary to point out the inferiority of professionals as compared to the 'gentleman players' of Slowcum Podger.

The inhabitants of Slowcum Podger generally are proud of their cricket club, and few events of the year so interest the old folks and wildly agitate the bosoms of the youngsters as the great annual match between Slowcum Podger and Mudcombe. As the affair comes off to-day, and Greek is to meet Greek in a few minutes on the village green, the excitement is already tremendous. This being Saturday, the so-called weaker sex is strongly represented, but though the ladies of Slowcum Podger pretend to be vastly interested in the pending struggle they really do not care one straw about it. In their hearts they detest this idiotic running between the wickets, and they get very indignant indeed when, the ball happening to come their way, there is a roar of 'get out of the road' raised by fielders and spectators alike. As if they wanted the ball! But for young Snooks, who in private life is rather a wild dog, to come bullying them for stopping it, is just a little bit too much. In short, the beauty of Slowcum Podger hate cricket matches because on those occasions, and on those occasions only, they are considered, at the best, persons of secondary importance. In the opinion of some young ladies – but this is mere assumption – it is, however, better to be sworn at than to be altogether ignored, and if Snooks only offers them a malediction it is preferable to the 'cutting' they receive at the hands of Slipper. If they only knew it, the kind of 'cutting' Slipper is thinking of has nothing to do with women, for Slipper is not only captain of the club, he is the craftiest run getter in Slowcum Podger, and his 'cutting' is the wonder of every school-boy who sees him at the wicket. Already has Slipper measured the 'pitch' and critically examined the 'crease', and now he and the captain of the Mudcombe players are tossing for first innings. Amid an awful silence the copper falls to the ground, and a ringing cheer immediately announces that Slipper – extraordinary clever fellow, Slipper! – has won the toss, and means to send his men in first. The Mudcombe players hide their chagrin by running to the wickets and having a little private bowling practice until the match proper commences, and some of their opponents come a little nearer to see how the renowned Slinger sends in the ball, and to judge whether he is in good form to-day, and has ground that will suit his curious delivery.

Meanwhile Slipper has written down the order in which the Slowcum Podger players are to go in, and as they have not heard the matter settled more than a hundred times already, they are crowding very anxiously round the scoring-sheet. Of course Swiper and Blocker are to go in first, that is the recognised thing in Slowcum Podger, and equally, of course, they do not get their pads on before Slipper has given them a number of those 'tips' which would be as useful as they are freely presented if they were ever acted on, which, it is hardly necessary to say, they never are. Blocker is a safe man, but the great difficulty about Swiper is that he too often gets bowled before he has had time to settle down. Once Swiper has settled down, as every male in Slowcum Podger can tell you, there is no getting him out, and, in the last match in which he played, over 80 runs went down to his account before he was accidentally snapped at the wickets. On the other hand he had been bowled without scoring a number of times that proved him a brilliant player rather than safe. Now, however, he and Blocker are padded and gloved, and if Slipper persists in giving them any more advice the enemy must get the advantage of it too, for the two batsmen are on their way to the wickets, Swiper smashing the daisies with his bat as he strides along, Blocker calm, unostentatious, chewing a blade of grass as is his wont. 'Ready?' asks the umpire. Everyone is ready, and the first ball is bowled. It goes to Swiper, who, remembering Slipper's last word, blocks it carefully, the next ball passes him without doing any damage, and then Swiper begins to hit out. 'Two and a one for Swiper,' shout the delighted spectators, convinced that their champion is about to give the Mudcombe players a rare day's leather-hunting. But their encouragement is ill-timed. It has made Swiper lose any head he ever possessed, and in the third over he 'skies' a ball

[21]

instead of driving it, as was, of course, his intention, out of the green. It falls into the bowler's hands, and Swiper retires covered with ignominy. How transitory a thing is popularity! When Swiper ran up his eighty the spectators cheered him to the echo, and there were not half-a-dozen of them who would not willingly have made him drunk at their own expense. But to-day he has been unlucky (hand slipped, he says), and the very schoolboys who would on the former occasion have gone down on their knees for a word from him now pass him by without a look. As for Slipper, he looks Swiper over contemptuously from head to foot and turns from him as if he knew him not. The vacant place is filled by Sly, who though, as already mentioned, long past his best days, is still a stubborn batsman, and he and Blocker run up the score to 20 before the latter is given out leg before. Slipper has only time to fling a reproachful word at the retiring batsman before he himself buckles to the fray, for the captain is going in now, and must keep his wind for hitting. There is a great deal in the way a man walks to the wickets, and Slipper's proud not to say haughty manner of stalking over the turf has ere this struck terror into the hearts of his opponents. When he reaches the wickets he has to make a new block hole and to flatten the turf on which his keen eye has detected an impudent buttercup, and then, after rearranging his cap and taking one brief look round the field, Slipper is ready. The next moment the captain of the Slowcom Podger cricket club wishes he could sink into the ground, for, owing to the most extraordinary combination of circumstances, Slinger has taken his off stump first ball. Looking like a collar with all the starch out of it, the discomfited captain retires with affected indifference, and, when he reaches the pavilion, ironically takes off his cap in acknowledgment of the applause no one offers to give. But from that moment until the tenth wicket falls, Slipper does nothing but button-hole his fellow-players to describe how it all happened, and he and Swiper become friends over their similar misfortunes. The Slowcum Podgers make some seventy runs in all, which in the country is considered not such a bad score, and it is evident, by the way the Mudcombe players whisper to each other when it is their turn to go in, that they are by no means confident of victory. It is not necessary to listen to their hopes and fears, for Mudcombe is only a second edition of Slowcum Podger, and,

[22]

whichever wins the day, there is still a great consolation left for the other. If it had not been for the victor's good luck it would easily have been defeated, so that the conquered eleven has really gained a 'moral victory'. Besides, the victorious team need not boast, for it will be annihilated next year.

Hippomenes, *Nottingham Journal*, 2 July 1883

The article shows many signs of being prepared and delivered in haste – not surprisingly – and of Barrie's comparative technical immaturity in his craft at this stage of his career. In the *Journal* a few weeks earlier, he had displayed (or had he?) all the emotional immaturity as well as the intolerance of most young men within an article entitled 'The Leafy Month'. 'In June, the cricketer shows what he is made of; if he does not make some good scores this month then had he better go and hang himself, for his season's average will certainly be low and he who can be happy with a poor average does not deserve the name of cricketer.'

Barrie was soon aware that the future of the *Nottingham Journal* was extremely precarious; there were rival papers operating and rumours that the *Journal*'s proprietors wanted to close down. As the principal literary contributor he was in a far more vulnerable position than that of most of his fellow reporters, for syndicated material could be bought in for less than his monthly salary. He applied, unsuccessfully, for a job at the *Liverpool Daily Post* and also started to test the London market. Inevitably and finally the axe fell, the *Nottingham Journal* no longer required his services and so he 'low-tailed' it back to Kirrie in somewhat sombre mood.

2

CRICKET IN ST JAMES'S

FREDERICK GREENWOOD, editor of the *St James's Gazette*, had expressed an interest in an *Auld Licht* article that Barrie had sent to the paper and soon was receiving more of the same. The young Scotsman had no doubt that London needed his services as a free-lance writer and wrote to Greenwood, asking should he leave the provinces and come to the big city. 'He was certain that he could manage, if necessary, on as little as a pound a week. If, then, the editor would give the matter his kind attention, his decision should be as final as on anything else.' 'No,' said Greenwood; so Barrie came.

Once in London, Barrie began to bombard Greenwood with the products of his elastic mind. In *The Greenwood Hat* – a memoir of some of Barrie's early scribing as James Anon and titled as such in honour of the silk or lum hat as they were called, bought, supposedly, to impress the great editor in their first face to face meeting – produced nearly fifty years later, Barrie adopts his *alter ego* and recalls the record of those times.

A Bibliography of his doings in this period finds some seventy articles in the 'St James's', nearly all of which, though they were of course unsigned, I seem to recognize by their titles, though the very skilful compiler, Mr Herbert Garland, can have had nothing to guide him save the British Museum or ancient files. I know of as many more, so this makes at least a hundred and forty accepted in these two years. I am sure that far more than twice that number had the sadder fate of rejection, though the second year gave Anon much more reason to rejoice than the first. Greenwood must have had at least four hundred hurled at him by the fast bowler, Anon.

Inevitably, there were a number about cricket. Titles such as 'The Cricket Spell', 'Boy on Lady Cricketers', 'Australian Cricketers' and 'The Season's Cricket' percolate his manuscripts – ideas and drafts for articles, some of which were never published. Happily some were, though for a slightly pompous London evening paper that took itself very seriously, Barrie pretended a solemn mien.

PREPARING FOR THE COMING TOPIC
(by one who is tired of it)

What I should do at this season of the year without my little nephews I hardly know. I get them to come to me as often as their educational studies permit; and it needs but a hint – and needs that but rarely – to start them on the subject of cricket. For now the cricket season has begun; and their much-informing talk is of 'cutting', 'cover-point', 'long-slip'; the 'slogging' of A, the comparative staleness of C, D, and E; and the sad frequency with which F is 'taken off his pads'.

To all this do I incline mine ear, and yet as one that heareth not. For thus is information most subtly imbibed; and I must, I must not fall behind in current cricket. Nothing whatever do I know of it at first hand, and, what is more, believe myself incapable of learning. But my second-hand information, artfully made the most of, gives me authority wheresoever two or three Englishmen are gathered together during the summer months. I am now in a position to pronounce a confident and racy forecast of the season. I can assure Yorkshire that their bowling is always in danger of getting tied in a knot, though I do not know exactly what it means. It is clear to me that the prospects of Notts are very good, though they are sorely in need of a 'trundler', and it is certain that 'Alf' has passed his best. 'Arthur' is as crisp as ever; but 'Billy' is a long time in getting into form, and there is some one who is a stone-waller. It is pleasant to be able to say decisively that he is a stone-waller, for 'stone-waller' is a good word; but some day I shall be asked what is a stone-waller, and then I fear me that I shall look extremely foolish.

During the days of a great match at Lord's or the Oval I am on the outlook for the boys long before they appear; for I know what will be the subject of conversation at dinner after the ladies have retired (or before); and when Billy is mentioned I hope to be able to remark carelessly, 'Oh, Billy, he was snapped at the wickets, you know'; or, 'he left to a bumpy one of Maurice's'; or, 'he popped one into George's hand because the wicket kicked': (while the wicket was kicking Billy could hardly be expected to show his usual form). The effect is instantaneous, and they settle down after that to listen to me with respect. But the worst of it is I am not able to follow up my advantage. While it lasts it is gratifying, but some day I shall be found out.

One should perhaps have a soul above cramming cricket, and well I know how sad is the consciousness of being a living lie. And yet if I did not cram I feel that I should be nowhere. In my heart I loathe the very name of cricket; but what would have been my lot last summer, for instance, when we had the Australians with us, if I had not been able to talk intelligibly to every one but myself about them? I shudder to think of it. My only sympathizer would have been the politician who telegraphed from his club for news of the doings in the Lords one night, and got for answer: 'Lord's, Australians 180 for five wickets; Murdoch 67, not out'. Last year there was a fever in the land – an epidemic brought over from the colonies; and if you did not suffer from it no one had any interest in you. On 'Change, in the lobbies of the House, in the mazes of the dance, in the streets, at the seaside, it was all the same. As well try to run away from oneself as to escape it. Early in June it broke out among the ladies, and there were some very serious cases. Lord Beaconsfield did not think the political utterances of the softer sex were to be taken seriously; and when one of them would have discussed with him some State secret of which she was not yet aware he deftly put her off with the remark that she was a little darling. But Lord Beaconsfield's lot was in easier times than these. Ladies have given up politics for cricket, and by the time the Australians return they may know something about it. And yet this summer, I learn from the papers, cricket is to be less the topic of the day, the colonists not being here to fire our patriotism. I would fain believe it. But that terrible eleven left behind it the germs of the epidemic in its worst form, and I see signs of its breaking out already. This summer – I feel it – will be spent in acquiring information. Fogies will be reading up the subject in a scientific handbook; the

[26]

play of Billy and the others will be criticised from a loftier standpoint than ever; there will be columns in the papers about how George has cut his thumb and Tom has turned sulky; and the slang will be more extraordinary and harder to get up than ever. The ladies will discover that the 'out' side do not change their places in the field according as they wish to be in the vicinity of certain fair spectators, and that the batsmen retire to the pavilion less frequently than you might think merely to give other players a chance. Last year I overawed them by calling the Australians 'corn-stalkers'; but it is impossible to keep up long at that level.

Let us not forget, however, that England does owe much of her greatness to her love for field sports, and the minority must suffer for the good of the greater number. And yet how I used to enjoy my summers before this craze took hold of people! Being a bookish man, I would go to a friend's house and talk about literature by the hour; but nowadays he yawns unless the books I mention are by Lillywhite. I would not grumble if the cricket gossip was confined to the ground itself. I would cheerfully let mankind exult over a 'lob' of Harry's or a 'pretty one' by Billy, if they would forget about it on the way home. But I will grieve no more. After all, I've much to be thankful for, even for those boys.

St James's Gazette, 16 May 1885

Barrie soon dropped his adopted pose. Within a couple of weeks he had resurrected a favourite rural theme.

CRICKET AT OUR VILLAGE

The cricketers of Wick-on-the-Green temper their enthusiasm with discretion, and know better than to lay the village common with turf. When an eleven accustomed to ground as true as a billiard-table comes to play them, it sneers at the ruts and lumps that twist a ball in spite of itself, and asks how scientific cricket is to be played at the bottom of a basin. At that the men of Wick-on-the-Green rub their hands and look slyly to the veteran Robb, who, however, manages to keep a grave face. He reserves his smiles of triumph for by-and-by.

[27]

When the enemy go to the wicket, Robb, craftiest of slow bowlers, who could easily be a professional if he liked, means to surprise them; and with the assistance of the bumpy ground, with which he is as familiar as a man with his sweetheart's face, he generally does.

There are many things connected with town cricket – 'drawing-room cricket' Robb calls it – which Wick-on-the-Green does not profess to understand. How you can take your ten minutes' practice, for instance, in front of a large net with half-a-dozen bowlers and no one fielding, is a mystery. We have matches among ourselves whenever as many as half-a-dozen of us get together on the green, and as these are always for glory and sometimes for a leg of mutton the excitement among players and spectators is very great. Owing to a variety of circumstances, we have not yet seen our way to erecting a pavilion; but on Saturdays we pitch a tent in the three-cornered wood that fringes the common on the east side, and the scorers are provided with a table. The club being of long standing, our fame is not inconsiderable; indeed, it is not many years since delegates from the county cricket committee paid us a visit (disguised as ordinary persons) on the occasion of our great annual encounter with Maggot-ponds – for the purpose, it was generally believed, of taking stock of our play. We did not do so well as usual that day, and so nothing came of it; but even when the delegates were afar off they are said to have expressed surprise at the number of persons journeying to the ground to witness the contest, as well as at the noise and hum that was borne to them from the green.

Such jealousy as that between Wick-on-the-Green and Maggot-ponds is scarcely known, even to rival actresses. During the winter it slumbers, despite an occasional football match or the like; but in the beginning of May it wakes like a giant refreshed, and rushes to the wickets. The contest should be a bi-yearly event, the return match taking place toward the end of the season; but at the first meeting there is generally a difference on some point of detail connected with the umpire's ruling, and the two elevens stalk from the ground in opposite directions. One of them at least – but generally both – claims the victory; and, as they part in dudgeon never to meet again, it is frequently a year before they make it up. One knowing in the ways of Wick-on-the-Green would not require to be told when the day of the great match comes round. The village shops, of which there are several, remain open,. it is true, but only for the convenience of enthusiasts in cricket: the trade being almost entirely confined to a roll spread with treacle, for which Wick-on-the-Green has some notoriety, and with which the spectators will sit out the game from its opening to its close.

The match of the season can also be known, after the introductory hubbub and boasting have subsided, by the comparative quietness of the spectators and the pallor of the players. Robb is a man whom not even Fisher of Maggotponds in his best form can terrify; but he has never quite succeeded in educating his team out of nervousness, and to-day they give way a little at the legs. Following a custom that is not popular in county matches, the side that wins the toss with us nearly always sends its opponents in first; and Stonewall and Power of the Wick Eleven, Robb having lost the toss (and having immediately gone down just a very little in the popular estimation in consequence), are now putting on their pads. Robb arranged the order of going in weeks ago, and hardly a man or boy on the green but would drop it from the point of his tongue if he opened his lips; yet an anxious multitude gape over the scorers' shoulders at the interesting row of names. When the village's two first representatives stalk to the wicket, Power mowing the daisies with his bat as he strides along and Stonewall chewing a straw, an uncanny silence prevails. Round the fielders Wick-on-the-Green squats itself tailor fashion, and only after Stonewall has returned the first three balls does it draw breath. The first over is a maiden, and now Power's turn has come. Wheresoever Wick-on-the-Green is known, there has Power's reputation for hard hitting penetrated; but not always does he make a score, for he is a reckless swiper and seldom settles down before he has had a 'life'. For the moment every eye is upon him, and that is a bad thing for Power.

Next moment the silence is broken by a 'How's that?' from eleven mouths, and Power is on his way back to the tent. Foot slipped, he says. A transitory thing is popularity. The boys who five minutes ago would have considered it an honour to be cuffed by Power now pass him by in silence. He goes and sits by himself on the fence. Next Robb is given out. Not bowled, you may be sure, for Maggotponds is

[29]

not so clever as that, nor was Robb the crafty ever known to 'sky' a ball. The fact is that an unfair umpire has given our captain out l.b.w. There is a roar of indignation from the crowd, and a clustering round the wickets. For a time it looks as if Maggotponds had better run for its life. But no one is exactly surprised, for no one in Wick remembers a match in which Robb got a fair chance; and no one who has come to Wick to play remembers Robb retiring to the tent without protesting against the umpire's ruling. On this occasion he demonstrates all round the green, using an umbrella as a bat, that his leg was not in a line with the wicket when he was given out; that even if it had been it would not have mattered, for the ball did not strike his leg at all; and other surprising things which grow upon him as he thinks about them.

Darker grow the brows of the men of Wick. Mr Norfor, the curate, who goes in second wicket down, puts on two pads, sends to the village for gloves, requests the wicket-keeper to pull a strap tighter, asks the one umpire to change hats with him and the other to give him a new block to himself, looks around thoughtfully to see where he had better hit, and is then bowled first ball. Fortunately for Wick-on-the-Green, an interesting feature in our cricket is that the worst player generally makes the heaviest score, and it is from this day that Munroe dates his fame. Munroe, whom Robb can take twice in an over, and who goes in last man, actually saves the game! While Power, who has been sung in verse, sits disconsolate on the fence, and the sad curate locks away his pads, and Driver the tremendous is telling Stonewall how he would have been in at this moment had not the bat turned round in his hands, and Stonewall is telling Driver where he fully intended to put the fatal ball, Munroe the despised is hitting Fisher all over the ground.

With us play begins at noon, and we do not draw the stumps until it is too dark to see. We do not fritter away three days in a single match, for with us three days means three matches; and yet the contest with Maggotponds seldom ends in a draw. I suppose the reason why we never make sensational scores is because our bowling is so deadly. Not for me is it to tell how this year Maggotponds went to the wickets with 54 to get to win, how the sun blazed into their eyes as punishment for their treatment of Robb, how Mr Norfor bowled the widest ball that was ever bowled by a Christian, and Stonewall, making an amazing leap into the air, caught the visitors' crack bat with his left hand. These are details that modesty shuns repeating. But go to Maggotponds and ask them how they fared that day at Wick-on-the-Green, or come to Wick-on-the-Green and fight the battle over again with Robb and Power. The accounts will vary, but you will at least learn that mighty deeds were done that day, though you may be uncertain which side did them. Then pass on to the green and learn, while the sun is going down, the hold that cricket has on a village people who do not have a professional (because they don't require one), and only know about 'gate money' from the newspapers.

St James's Gazette, 27 May 1885

A year later, in the pages of the *Gazette*, Barrie recapitulated on the topic of which he had pretended to be tired.

BOYS AT CRICKET

There are few pleasanter sights in this world than a stretch of green on a sunny day, with two-and-twenty little boys working at cricket on it. It is only after mixing among them that you get to know what a serious pastime cricket is. On the other hand, an adult never feels quite such a poor creature as when, being perhaps their instructor in the dead languages, he consents to join in the game, knowing nothing about it. He may have a surprising acquaintance with irregular verbs, but that does not save him if he puts his legs where his bat should be. 'Out!' says the umpire sternly – a young gentleman in a long overcoat, holding a bat nearly the length of himself, who has stuck for a month at 'Balbus builds a wall; Caius flies from the city'. A smile of derision is passed round the field; your captain, aged twelve, waves you out of the way; cheeky little Lewis says, 'Another duck's egg, sir!' You retire gloomily to the fence, and sit neglected, deserted, forgotten.

A man may be a good teacher and a gentleman, though he has not the least idea how to play a 'full-pitched one'. Any honourable boy

[31]

will admit that. But then, he should not play cricket. He should have strength of character to resist the voice of the wheedler, who may be the head master or only the cocky little captain. The one wishes him to take part in the games in order to exercise a general superintendence; the other is probably actuated by no more worthy motive than a desire to make him ridiculous. The weak teacher yields to his flatterers in spite of his better judgment. 'Swiping' looks so easy, and so it is if the balls do not come in straight. So he becomes a member of the first eleven. If he is a cricketer, well and good; but to be the worst player in the team is to fling away your reputation as a superior creature. In the field you are no longer 'Mr Gilbert', but only 'backstop', and your captain calls you 'tenth wicket'. If you are acute of hearing you soon know that your nickname is 'Butter-fingers'. I have spoken above, possibly with a certain bitterness, of 'full-pitched ones'. It was a full-pitched one that revealed me to our school in my true form. I had been sent in second wicket down as an experiment, and it looked at first as if I were a born cricketer. My play astonished myself more than any other person. I had no idea cricket was so easy. All I did was to shut my eyes and, as Lewis put it afterwards, 'blaze away'. In that first over I made seven runs. Then the captain of the opposing team, who had been narrowly watching my play said aloud that he saw 'the way to do me'. He was bowling, and he pitched the ball high, nicely calculating that if I missed it it would alight on the wicket. I did miss it, and out I went. That was a 'full-pitched' one. It is considered particularly contemptible to be beaten by a full-pitched one.

The boy cricketer leaves nothing to chance. Hours before the enemy appear he is on the ground 'rolling' the 'pitch', marking out the crease, and knocking down the still smaller boys who stand upon the chalk. It is a sight to see our captain directing the pitching of the wickets. He has long ago convinced his eleven that his stride is an exact yard. If the standard measure were lost he would come in handy. So he struts what he calls twenty-two yards in twenty-two steps, and that is our pitch. If the eleven had any sense of humour on the cricket-ground, they would nickname him Bantam. But in point of fact the whole school is lost in admiration of that boy. The day he made forty-two in as many minutes the head master took his arm and walked round the field with him. Other small boys followed at a respectful distance, and noted that Crowder was perfectly at his ease. He let out subsequently, in the course of conversation, that he had 'chaffed' the head master on quite a personal matter, and that the head master had seemed rather pleased. Some of the boys believed this, and some of them did not. It was, however, generally acknowledged that Crowder had borne himself well. On another occasion he was invited to tea by the head master's wife, and asked her in the coolest manner possible to pass the butter. Such stories as these, though mostly given to the world on Crowder's own authority, are considered a credit to the school. In the playground they make him a little bumptious. There is not a 'man' in the eleven who would not rather have a word of praise from Crowder about his 'play' than take a hundred per cent. in an examination on the subjunctive mood. When his side is in, Crowder sits apart from the common herd, with other boys to bear messages from him to his 'men'. A big hit is rewarded with a 'Well driven, sir!' from Crowder, and then every one cheers.

Crowder takes note of everything. He knows the weaknesses of his team even better than their strength, and is always ready with a word of warning. 'Cautious, young Roberts!' is his shout to the 'swiper' who has made a leg-hit for three, and has rather lost his head in exultation over it. Every man in the eleven goes to Crowder for final instructions just before he goes in; and though he forgets them the next moment in his excitement, it is well known that Crowder's hints are worth following. Jones is warned not to 'run out of his ground'. Well, Jones forgets to keep this advice at heart; and as a result you will see that he is 'stumped'. Then there is Wilkinson, who has a reputation for making a big score 'once he settles down'. The difficulty with Wilkinson is that he is nearly always out before he has had time to settle down. Crowder presses upon him to 'play back' for an over or two, and Wilkinson promises, but doesn't. Smithers, on the other hand, 'lets out' at straight balls and misses them. He can drive every other kind of ball all over the field; but straight balls are as fatal to him as full-pitched ones are to me. It is not Crowder's way to 'chaff' a man who, from not following his advice, retires from the wickets in disgrace: he simply ignores him. And to be treated with silent contempt by Crowder is terrible. You go and sit down beside

[33]

him to explain that the ball was quite unplayable, and he turns round and addresses some one else. At such a time Crowder thinks nothing of telling a boy half as big again as himself to 'shut up'. There is, it is true, occasional muttering against Crowder – that is, when he has been unfortunate himself. Crowder does not always make forty-two. Sometimes he is even out for a 'duck', and then he goes all round the field explaining that the whole thing was an accident. Crowder is a great stickler for etiquette in the field, and has a deaf ear for all complaints from his men that the umpire has given them out unfairly. Nevertheless, there is a tremendous row when Crowder is given out l-b-w or 'run out' himself. When our side is in the field he rules as with a rod of iron, though a smart return is generally rewarded with an approving word. I get very red in the face and bite my lips myself when I fling in the ball wide; and, though it is, perhaps, a humiliating thing for a master to say, I feel intensely gratified when he rewards me with a careless 'Well fielded, Back-stop!'

Boys have a code of honour of their own to which they adhere more or less strictly; but it is a code not understood by adults, and has frequently put me in an awkward position. It allows of much deceit in the cricket-field. For instance, when our second eleven travels to Pulsford Hall to play the second eleven there, it is not our genuine second eleven at all. Crowder, of course, does not play on such occasions, for the fame of Crowder has reached far; but several others of the first eleven do. There is Green, a first-eleven man known as 'Kilty', because he wears a kilt. It is not considered dishonourable to put Kilty into trousers and send him to Pulsford Hall under another name as a genuine member of the second eleven. Then French, who also plays in that capacity, is merely a boy in the village with a reputation for bowling. French looks 'one of us' in Mullins's flannels, and he is put up to saying to the Hall eleven that though not a boarder at our school he comes to it for lessons in German. Crowder had the audacity to ask me to teach French a German sentence which he could fire off at the Hall boys as a proof of his genuineness. On my refusing, French was instructed to say 'hundert' through his nose at short intervals; and he does it so frequently, and with such a barefaced disregard for the first letter that I am always surprised the

Hall players do not find him out. They detected Kilty some time ago.

St James's Gazette, 4 June 1886

Already, in his early manhood, Barrie's predilections for an avuncular role can be detected – not that one should attempt to define the attitudes of such a complex character as Barrie in such simplistic terms; nevertheless, when one aligns his feelings for children to his acute awareness of the reactions of women, particularly in their response to games ('I soon grow tired of writing tales unless I can see a little girl, of whom my mother has told me, wandering confidently through the pages,' he wrote), it is hardly surprising both feature to an uncommon degree in his work. Some thoughts in his note-books are revealing: 'Boy upholds tutor. He made 77 not out – should marry a girl.' 'Schoolboy. A Cricket Match in which a lady plays. The men favour her to boy's indignation – or it never strikes him that they cd. do such a thing.'

The article that appeared in the *Gazette* during the summer of 1885, however, concentrated on just one side of the equation.

LADIES AT CRICKET

One hot forenoon in this month of July I lay on the edge of a green field beneath a cherry-tree, the idle spectator of a cricket match between a ladies' school and eleven young women of the neighbour-hood. Not long before I had seen two teams of the softer sex scrimmaging over a football – hardly an edifying spectacle. But here they made a pretty picture, those young girls flitting about in print and flannel, and the field was vocal with their chatter. The elevens wore at their waists a rose – a red rose the girls, the others a Marshal Niel; and the victorious side were to leave the field with the rose of the vanquished at their belts.

The sides tossed for first innings without giggling in the least; but, owing to a little peculiarity of one of the captains, who could not toss the coin without flinging up both her arms and jerking it over her head, several coins were lost in the grass before this point was settled. Then the Marshal Niels went to the wickets, carrying their bats beneath their arms; while the 'out' side gathered round the crease to

[35]

hem in the ball and have a little chat until it happened to come their way. The first representatives of the yellow rose were Miss Rawlins and Miss Thoms (who were loudly cheered on going to the wickets), and the attack was entrusted to Miss Mitchell (swift daisy-cutters) and a tall girl familiarly addressed as 'Georgie' (medium lobs). The first over was a maiden, but off Georgie's second ball Miss Rawlins scored 1; following it up shortly afterwards by lifting Miss Mitchell smartly to the on for 2. Runs now came slowly. Miss Thoms gave point a chance of a hard one, which was not taken, and then skied Georgie straight above mid-wicket, amid much cheering. For this 1 was recorded. Several singles and a bye followed, and then Miss Mitchell found her way to Miss Rawlins's wicket (one for 11). The next comer was Miss Philips, who immediately opened out to a tempting one from Georgie, and put her away to leg for 3. For this only 2 should have been scored; but the fielder, instead of smartly returning the ball, ran with it to the wickets and put it personally into the wicket-keeper's hands. Off the next ball Miss Philips had a 'life' from Miss Welsh at point, who had the ball, but dropped it through some misunderstanding. This cost the 'out' side dear; for Miss Philips was now in grand form, and subjected the fielders to a rare piece of leather-hunting. Having driven Miss Mitchell for a brace, she stepped out to a wide one from the same bowler and lifted it grandly from the off to leg. In the next over she snicked one nicely through the slips, for which a couple was chronicled, and then, running after a wide, hit it hard behind the wicket-keeper. This brought on Miss Coombes, *vice* Georgie; but runs still came, and the score stood at 25 after three-quarters of an hour's play. The separation, however, was now effected. In stealing a run the two batswomen ran into each other, and before they could decide which side to take Miss Hibbert (mid-wicket) had hastened to Miss Coombes with the ball and told her what to do with it. Miss Philips was the smartly run out. She had played a merry innings of 14. (Two for 25.) Miss Empson, who came in second wicket down, did not seem at home with Miss Coombe's bowling, and, having slicked her in a rather fluky manner for 1, had her wickets spreadeagled by the following ball. (Three for 26.) Thirty was brought on soon afterwards in byes, no long-stop apparently being securable with sufficient courage to touch the ball until it stopped; while the wicket-keeper talked too much to slip. A change of bowling was again resorted to, Miss Hibbert taking the ball from Miss Mitchell, in the hope of getting another wicket before luncheon; but both batswomen played carefully, never hitting out except when they felt confident of raising the ball high in the air. When the bell rang the score stood at 34 – still for three wickets.

Play was resumed at 1.45, when the two not-outs (Miss Thoms, 7, and Mrs Gilmour, 0) faced the bowling of Miss Hibbert and Miss Mitchell. Off the former's third ball Miss Thoms – who was now playing with more confidence – should have scored a brace, getting a full-pitched one dead on the leg-wicket well away to cover-point; but Mrs Gilmour, making a mistake as to the place to which she had to run, rushed off in the direction of long-on and was run out. (Four for 34.) Further disaster befell the 'in' side in the next over, Miss Thoms knocking off the bails with the skirt of her dress three times. She was then given out. The retiring batswoman was loudly cheered, having played an invaluable innings of 7, the merit of the performance being far beyond the mere value in runs. In amassing this score Miss Thoms, who had not given a chance, had been at the wickets for an hour and a half. The bowling, though the ground was a little torn, was now dead on the spot, and run-getting was extremely difficult. At 36 Miss Mitchell dismissed Miss Curson with an unplayable one, pitched full on to the bails; and the two succeeding batswomen failed to score. (Six, seven, and eight for 36.) Mrs French, the next woman in, fell just as she was getting well set, and retired to change her dress. Things were now looking black for the Marshal Niels, but the last wicket gave a deal of trouble, and a change of bowling had to be again resorted to. Miss Leslie spanked Miss Hibbert hard for 2, and snicked the same bowler through the slips for 1, both hits being lofty and deservedly cheered. At 42 the tenth wicket was taken l-b-w, and the innings came to an end; Miss Leslie carrying out her bat for a superb 4, compiled without a vestige of a chance.

The innings of the Red Rose was opened by Miss Hibbert and Miss Wace, to the bowling of Mrs French and Miss Leslie. Miss Hibbert, who took the first over, hardly seemed at home with Miss Leslie, who has a dangerous delivery, pitching her balls so high that it is

[37]

extremely difficult to reach them. Off Mrs French's second over Miss
Wace drew one to square-leg, and Miss Hibbert, stepping out to a
tempting one of Miss Leslie's, drove it terrifically to the on for a
single. Ten soon went up amid loud cheering. The scoring now
became fast and furious, the batswomen obtaining a complete mastery of the bowling. Miss Wace getting under one of Miss French's,
lifted it over the bowler's head, where it might have been caught by
long-on had she thought of it in time. Miss Hibbert added a brace of
singles, and then Miss Wace made the hit of the day. Hastening after
a wide one from Miss French, which had gone in the direction of the
pavilion, she overtook it at square-leg and struck it a severe blow
from behind. Some idea of the velocity at which the ball travelled
may be gathered when it is said that five fielders were required to
bring it back. With the score at 20, Mrs Gilmour took the ball from
Mrs French, but was only allowed to bowl one over. Her delivery is
peculiar, but perhaps too slow; the batswoman having only to await
the coming of the ball to rest in the middle of the pitch, to propel it in
whatever direction she chooses. At 23, Miss Wace, in playing back,
hit her wicket, and the next comer failed to score. With two of the
best wickets down for 23, the prospects of the 'in' side were now less
bright. Miss Coombes played finely for 2; but was dismissed by a
brilliant catch at point, where she dropped the ball into Miss Leslie's
hands. This was the smartest bit of fielding of the match, and the
other players gathered round Miss Leslie to congratulate her. After a
short interval for conversation play was resumed, when Miss Hibbert
opened her shoulders to a short-pitched one from Mrs French and
lifted it grandly into the hands of cover-point. For this a couple was
scored. The result seemed a foregone conclusion with the score at 35
for two wickets; but a remarkable change came over the aspect of the
game when Miss Curson was put on to bowl. In her first over she did
the hat trick, her delivery being so swift that no defence was
attempted. With only five wickets to fall and 8 runs to get to win there
was still a possibility of the Marshal Niels pulling the match out of the
fire, and the fielding now became very smart and clean. The next over
was productive of neither runs nor wickets; but at 38 Miss Mitchell
was accidentally thrown out, and Miss Hume was bowled off her
dress without scoring – 7 for 38. The excitement was now keen, and

[38]

bets in gloves were freely offered and taken. By byes and singles the score rose slowly to 41, when Miss Mounsey was cleverly snapped at the wickets. Miss Curson had now gone completely off her form, and Mrs French was again tried. At 42 Miss Croall should have been run out, Mrs Gilmour bungling the ball. This lost the Marshal Niels the match, for at 5.30 Miss Croall made the winning hit, a deep one through the slips. The most successful bowlers on the winning side were Miss Curson, who took three wickets for 7 runs, and Miss Leslie (three wickets for 14 runs), who bowled consistently well throughout. Mrs French also trundled well. With the exception of Mrs Gilmour, the Marshal Niels fielded so smartly that it would be invidious to make distinctions.

St James's Gazette, 14 July 1885

When he came to compile *The Greenwood Hat*, Barrie refused to resist the temptation to make significant alterations to the original text for 'Ladies at Cricket'. By then, of course, he had considerably more time at his disposal and it is rewarding to read the later version, if only in order to see a mature writer's view of his early work (See Appendix p. 176).

Three years later in 1888 Barrie was still writing articles for Greenwood – by now, their relationship was based on firm friendship born of mutual respect – though during that summer the editor told his protégé that he was leaving the paper. The *Gazette* had changed hands and Greenwood did not see eye to eye with the new proprietor.

As the cricket season got under way, Barrie provided complementary articles on two protagonists.

THE FEELINGS OF A BOWLER
(by a Poet)

The feelings of a Bowler, how seldom are they considered! The sorrows of a Poet are respected, and Lord Tennyson has particularly requested the public not to trouble the Poet's mind. But what are they to the feelings of a Bowler (like Lord Byron)? I am a Poet myself, and a Bowler; and I have no hesitation in saying that the chords which vibrate in the bosom of the latter are infinitely more sensitive

[39]

than those which thrill the breast of the former. For, at worst, a Poet is merely neglected, or sniffed at by the gents who write the Minor Notices without cutting the pages of the books sent to them. But the Bowler hears with his ears the cry of 'Take him off!' and sees, occasionally, the lack of appreciation shown in the faces of the fields. What is a literary 'slating' compared to being hit for four fours in an over? Not that I blame the batsman – he acts after his kind; but the fielders, and the captain, and the public, occasionally – them I do blame. Besides, poetry is a mere pastime of the intellect; to bowl head balls – to bowl them well – requires a very different sort of mind and body. I lately read advice to batsmen, in which they were counselled to wait for a fast bowler's attempt at a slow head-ball (which is nearly certain to be bad) and then to let him have it! It may have been Dr Grace or Mr A. G. Steel who wrote these unfeeling words; I am sure it was no fast bowler.

The sensitive genius in other walks of art may not always 'come off'. If I were a painter, for example, I should hardly joy when the work of months was skied, and that in the New Gallery. But it is worse when one's pet head-ball is either not skied at all, but crumped along the ground for six; or is skied, and then dropped by a fellow who misjudges it, though it was hit into his hands in the very place you set him. I have a pet head-ball. The reflection of my waking hours was given to it for weeks, and I could nearly always bring it off – in practice. You begin your over with a good length ball, then you send in one rather short, but high in the curve, just good enough for the batter to find it is a trap and play back. The next looks the same, and is as high in the curve, but it is pitched almost a half-volley. The batsman (in practice) thinks this is the same ball as the one before and plays back again. Hence 'a row in his timber-yard', as Mr Bouncer said. But in a match he 'yanks' it round to broad field for as many as the nature of the boundary will permit him to score. Then think of the feelings of the bowler, especially if his captain comes up and suggests the need of a change!

It is a horrid thing to be taken off. Nobody likes it; and some bowlers, when captains, never take themselves off at all. 'An obvious instance,' as the crib to the *Ethics* says, 'will readily occur'; you feel as I fancy the author of *Treasure Island* may when everybody asks him if he has read *Robert Elsmere* – at least, that is how I feel. You can hardly take pleasure in the success of your side when the new man gets the wickets. An amateur once told me a horrid but credible instance of these sentiments. He was playing in a country match, and the professional bowler on his side failed to dislodge a sturdy opponent. The professional was taken off, my friend went on, and lowered the wickets in his first over. The professional then went stark staring mad on the spot (he had been a little off the spot before), and never recovered from the shock. Did anyone ever hear of the feelings of a poet carrying him so far?

I was present (an unworthy guest) at the dinner of the Royal Academy when Mr Lecky, that eminent authority on verse, praised Mr Robert Buchanan's new poems and said they were – I don't quite remember what, but I *think* he said as good as the classical pictures exhibited in the gallery. More than one poet was there besides myself – two other poets at least; and yet none of us had to be put in strait-waistcoats. We merely remarked that we shouldn't wonder. Yes; that poor untutored ground-bowler had far finer feelings, a far more frantic sense of envy, and less self-control than quite a choir of poets. But who cares, who ever dreams of sparing the feelings of a bowler? You may say, How could a captain win matches if he did? and there is something in that. Besides, of course, there are the other men yearning to be put on. I have not enumerated – who could? – the trials of a bowler. What a thing it is to have catches missed off one! My extreme Radical opinions I trace to the day when a batsman was missed off me four times in one over by a titled wicket-keeper, and several times at cover-point by a belted earl. But is that much worse than over-throws? A batsman makes a feeble push to short-leg. The field lets it go for one, buzzes it in frantically, wicket-keeper lets it go for four; and that four is against *you*, the bowler, in the analysis. They complain of bowlers trundling to keep down the runs; they say Mr Spofforth is the only man who bowls (like a cricketing General Grant) for wickets purely, at any cost of runs. Then Mr Spofforth must be a fellow of no delicacy, though his technical skill is undeniable. Perhaps the roughest thing for a bowler is when singles are made, nearly every ball, to short-leg and third man. These detestable fellows are *never* in the right place. Somehow the wonder is that

Bowlers are not misanthropes. For my part I attribute the spleen of Lord Byron to no other causes. What else had he to complain of? He bowled for Harrow; Eton beat them; and I dare say catches were missed off him. Cowper, too, was a poet and a cricketer – probably a bowler. *Hinc illæ lacrymæ.* Swift, as all the world knows, attributed his bad humour to losing a big trout when he was a boy and had nearly landed him. That, also, might well embitter a disposition for life; but it is less trying than getting the best Cambridge bat notoriously l-b-w in the first over, and having the umpire give him 'Not out', and then seeing him put on a century. But if a bowler once begins to talk about umpires! Enough has been said to show that the fine and subtle temperament of the Bowler is subjected to sorrows far exceeding those which make the Poet teach in song what he learned in suffering. And we, Bowlers I mean, are mute! We do not turn the agonies of our hearts into metrical copy, and revel in dozens of editions at a royalty. These consolations, which a successful Poet rejoices in – these pecuniary rewards of his regrets, his moans for dead friends and faithless young women – a Bowler would scorn to receive. *He* does not coin his heart-drops: he suffers and is still. That is why you never, hardly, meet elegant little volumes, named *Heart's Sorrows*, by Lohmann, or Briggs, or Mr Whitby, or Mr Christopherson. They are too manly to weep in public. My own *Elegies* (still in their first edition) are about agonies I never felt half so much as I feel being 'collared'. 'Collared!' the very word is like a knell!

St James's Gazette, 17 May 1888

THE FEELINGS OF A BATSMAN
(by a Proser)

I am no Poet, and very little of a Bowler; and, to speak truth, neither my prose nor my batting has ever been thought first-rate. I am conscious, therefore, of being sadly hampered (like a batsman with a man to run for him) in following the accomplished Poet-Bowler who has had his innings before me. What are pads against a Poet? What rectitude of purpose (though rectitude of bat be well) against a Bowler? Glorious combination! To be a Poet is much: to be a Bowler

[42]

is more. There are poets nowadays piping from every garret; but bowlers, they tell us, are scarce. Happy man! his own generation is proud of him, and lang – I mean long shall posterity cherish his memory as of one who, like the old Timon, 'greatly daring, greatly broke'. But I am getting wide; did I not say I was no Bowler?

To come to the point – and I was never much good there – has a batsman no feelings? I maintain him to be more despitefully used than any bowler. Take one case only. The batsman is out, perhaps bowled or caught first ball, perhaps unjustly dismissed by a cruel, a careless, or a cross-eyed umpire: such things have been. His chance is over. Man – the batting-man – 'gets no second day', at least not in that innings, though in the next he may haply fetch up past opportunities. But the bowler bowls on. If he be captain of his side, he may bowl on for ever. A little boy wrote the other day triumphantly to his father of a match in which his school had been engaged. 'I was captain,' he wrote, 'and so bowled all the time.' Excellent little boy! He has the makings of a Grace in him. But think of the poor batsman. He goes in first, big with high thoughts of 'all the centuries yet to come' – and out first. His companions build up a huge score; but there he sits, not conquering but conquered, under the cool shade of the pavilion, musing over a mis-spent existence. What can he do? No one cares to hear his explanations. If he takes up an afternoon newspaper, he is sure to spy his own discomfiture writ large in the cool malignity of print; he is shamed to stroll round the ground to look up old friends. The sun shines, the air shakes with plaudits; but not for him.

Consider, again, a batsman, the hero of his side, after whom, through all the term at Oxford or Cambridge, at Eton or Harrow, the panting scorers have been toiling in vain: consider him going in, second wicket down, the common place for your champion. Gaily he steps out into the sunlight, amid loud expectant cheers. He walks to the wicket, takes his guard, picks a stray fragment of grass or so off the pitch, looks round the field, settles his cap on his head, and – What means that tremendous shout, that after-silence yet more tremendous? What figure is this returning feebly, like Hampden from Chalgrove Field, with his head down, listless? No mere bowler can ever know the anguish of that moment. A friend of mine once

[43]

bowled from early morn to dewy eve on the third day of the University match. Nobly he bowled, as eight wickets remain on Lillywhite's pages to this day to testify. But 'twas heart-breaking work. His field, unlike the Sultan's falcon, *did* let go what they once clutched. One, my friend has often assured me (he has a pretty fancy) missed three catches off every over. Yet, allowing the usual reduction on a quantity, what were my bowling friend's feelings to those of the baffled hero which I have feebly essayed to picture?

The other day at Oxford Mr J. G. Walker made ninety-nine runs, and carried out his bat. What are ninety-nine runs? As well make none as fall one short of the coveted hundred. What must be his feelings towards the man at the other wicket who defrauded him of his just triumph! They had been friends before, very like, with a friendship cemented on many a well-fought field. They can never be so again. Some thin pretence of friendship may still be kept between them, but no more.

I remember (shall I ever forget it?) a college match in the prehistoric days of my youth. We played an eleven of our predecessors, a particular match to inaugurate our new ground. After lunch the two elevens were photographed in front of the pavilion. The most conspicuous object in that photograph was (nay, is – I saw it t'other day!) the telegraph-board; the most conspicuous object on that telegraph-board is an 'o', recording the score of the last wicket. That 'o' is mine! I suffered many checks many bad moments during my career at the university; but their memory has grown dim. I can laugh at them now: at this only I cannot laugh. It is ever rising before me. I go to pass a happy evening with an old college friend, to 'talk o'er old talks, play as we used to play'. On his table lies an album. I open it: there are they all, 'the old familiar faces'. Then I turn a page, and lo! the accursed thing! No mere bowler can ever be thus 'damned to everlasting fame'.

Think also on the position of a batsman. He is one against so many. There is the bowler, and the ten hungry fieldsmen against him – nay, and the two umpires into the bargain, maybe. Think, too, of the insults we have sometimes to endure: a field called contemptuously in, the studied insolence of 'silly point', the perpetual aggravation of that monster behind us, 'the padded man who wears the gloves', his unwarrantable liberties with our bails, the damnable iteration of his appeals to the umpire, his 'windy suspirations of forced breath' at hair-breadth 'scapes which the poor victim cannot repudiate. A good wicket-keeper is the most offensive of created beings.

These, however, are only the spiritual troubles of a batsman, and of such even a bowler may, I grant, have his share. But consider our corporeal griefs. This Poet-Bowler talks of the agony of being 'collared'. What is that to the agony of being 'cut over'? A bowler is never 'cut over'; at least he has only himself to thank if he is: he can take himself out of the way of any inconvenient ball, and (I speak as a batsman) is a fool if he do not. But the batsman must abide the shock. The most timorous or the most strong-minded will hardly dare to 'run away' when the eyes of his school, his university, or his country are on him. Let the bowling be never so fierce, the wicket never so fiery, the batsman must, like Major Gahagan, be found at his post. And when the ball finds him there! 'O what labour! O Prince, what pain!' The bowler groans at the misery of getting a man out leg-before-wicket in his first over when the umpire is not looking or looks to no proper purpose; but what is his misery to the misery of the man who owns the leg if the ball be a fast one?

These are some of the reasons, inadequately expressed, which make the batsman in my eyes a far more elegiac figure than any bowler can be. His joys, I grant, are proportionately greater, his moments of bliss more thrilling – the joy of bowling a good ball can obviously be nothing to the joy of hitting it – his triumphs more popular and enduring. But these I must leave another hand to record: here my personal experience fails me.

St James's Gazette, 31 May 1888

[45]

[3]

CRICKET WITH DISPATCH

AMONG the hundreds of articles that Gavin Ogilvy, James Anon and J. M. Barrie wrote for *St James's Gazette*, *British Weekly*, *Courant*, *Home Chimes*, *Illustrated London News*, *Pall Mall Gazette*, *National Observer* and a host of other journals, one wonders just how many were on cricket. After four years of extraordinary industry, Barrie's 'mild estimate' was over eight hundred pieces on all subjects, including many consigned to the waste-paper bin by either overworked or myopic editors. It is unlikely that amongst that number there were not a good few on his favourite topic; in one of his notebooks, for example, there is a line which reads: 'Charles Lamb essay on Allahakbarrie's Cricket'. Whether a piece in the style of Elia ever reached fruition, was rejected, printed or was lost, is not known, at least, to the present writer.

Alexander Riach, editor of the *Edinburgh Evening Dispatch*, a steadfast friend, whom he had met in London when Riach was working on the *Daily Telegraph*, provided another valuable outlet for Barrie's feverish activity. He never refused any article, even if it seemed to be of principal interest to those living within the environs of a seaside town in southern England.

A LADIES' CRICKET MATCH
(described by a Male Professional)

On the third of this month a cricket match between two elevens of ladies took place in a field near Eastbourne. These cricket contests between female teams are not at all uncommon on the south coast now during the summer months, but this one got into the papers chiefly because a Mrs Coombes made 42 for the winning side.

Happening to be staying at the fashionable watering-place, I was present during the greater part of the game, and though it did not strike me at the time to write a detailed account of it, the eagerness with which many of the papers published a very meagre report with comments, has persuaded me that the public is interested in these contests. Perhaps it is not too late in the day to describe the match still. As may be remembered, the one side was composed of summer visitors to Eastbourne, while its opponents were Eastbourne ladies. The former started a club some two months ago, and, it may be added, lent two players (the sisters Townley) to their opponents who found greater difficulty in getting up an eleven. I have been told that, to add to the interest of the game, it was agreed that the losing side should give the victors a box of chocolates, but I did not learn whether this was a fact.

In the field the Visitors presented a charming appearance. They wore white skirts with blue and white bodices, the latter held together at the waist with the orthodox cricket belt, and all had white and blue cricket caps. The other side were hardly so picturesque. They had not been able to agree on a costume, and had finally arranged that each should dress as she pleased. The result was that no two were attired precisely alike. Eastbourne won the toss after some delay caused by the penny's disappearance when flung into the air. This was because the captain of the Visitors, a lovely girl, with brown hair, always flung it behind her instead of tossing it straight up, and became hysterical with excitement lest it should strike her on the head as it came down. After three pennies had been tossed one of them was found on the grass. Nobody was sure which one it was, and the Eastbourne captain had called 'head' and 'tails' time about, but to waste no more of the day it was agreed that the Visitors had won the toss. After a little talk among themselves they agreed to send Eastbourne to the wickets.

The Eastbourne captain sent in Miss Lucy Townley and Mrs Coombes to face the bowling of Miss Frobisher (medium lobs), and Miss Katie Metcalf (slow twisters). Mrs Salmond kept wickets, and the other fielders stood in two groups – one on each side of the batswoman, glancing behind them every minute to see if any one was looking. Miss Metcalf took the first over, sending up a difficult one,

[47]

which Miss Townley lifted to point amid loud cheering. Her fourth ball went swiftly past the wicket-keeper, who ran after it with long-stop, and when it stopped picked it up, and flung it to Miss Frobisher, who stopped it with her foot. 'How's that?' called out Miss Frobisher. 'Out,' said the umpire (Mrs Wyatt). Here the game was interrupted, as the umpire could not decide which of the players was out. It was ultimately agreed that both should get another chance, and this decision cost the Outs dear, for in the next over Mrs Coombes lifted Miss Frobisher high to mid-wicket for 2, and then hit her smartly to leg for another brace. A smart piece of fielding here by Miss Lucy Wilson was loudly cheered. Running alongside the ball, she picked it up as soon as it had stopped, and flung it with both hands to the umpire, who held up her bat to the scorers to signify that Miss Wilson had scored one. Runs now came fast, Miss Townley opening out to a wide one from Miss Frobisher, and cutting it with all her force past point, while Mrs Coombes put Miss Metcalf away to long on for 2 and 3. As the batswomen seemed set, a change of bowling was tried, Miss White going on in place of Miss Frobisher. The separation, however, was effected from the other end, Miss Townley being clean bowled by Miss Metcalf for a capital 4. She had been at the wickets for seven minutes, her principal strokes being a 2 and 1 (one wicket for 11). The next comer was Miss Rogers, who fell when taking 'centre', and retired to change her dress (two for 11). Miss Tower followed, and opened by cracking Miss White to leg for 1, and then opening her shoulders to a short pitched one from the same bowler she pulled it to the off for 2. Miss Metcalf then found her way to Miss Tower's wicket (three for 14). Mrs Hastings then came in, and for a time the play was uneventful. Mrs Coombes made things lively by spanking two successive balls hard to the on for 3 and 4, and lifting Miss White over her head for a trio. Several singles followed, and 30 went up at twelve o'clock. At 34, a clever bit of fielding on the part of Miss Jenny Waters got rid of Mrs Hastings, who had been playing a cautious game. Miss Metcalf had sent up three balls, all of which were twisting dead on the wicket, but unfortunately stopped when they had got half way. Mrs Hastings ran out to the third of these, and before she could get back into her ground Miss Waters rushed at the wickets, and smartly knocked off the bails with her

[48]

hand. (4 for 34.) Miss Reid, the next comer, was neatly snapped at the wickets without scoring, but Miss Tompkins (known as the 'stonewaller') made a stand, leaving Mrs Coombes to do the scoring. Runs came slowly, both bowlers being now dead on the wickets. At 40, Miss Metcalf gave place to Miss Grainger (fast daisy-cutters). This lady bowls at such a terrific speed that, did the balls go straight she would capture six wickets in an over. Neither batswoman attempted to face her bowling, the plan adopted being to stand far away from the wickets, and then run as soon as the ball had passed them. Long-stop did not try to stop the ball until it was dead, and thus byes were registered with great rapidity. Fifty went up, and the Visitors' captain took the ball in the hope of obtaining another wicket before luncheon. The change proved effective. Having cut the new bowler through slip, Miss Tompkins started to run, but was detained by midwicket, who got in her way, and tried to push her back. Slip had in the meantime run with the ball to the wicket-keeper, who quickly pulled the wickets out of the ground, and then flung the ball behind her back. (6 for 53.)

After the adjournment for luncheon Mrs Coombes (31) and Miss Fern faced the bowling of Miss Metcalf and Miss Frobisher. The latter was exceedingly difficult to play, changing her style of bowling with every ball, but could get no wickets. Sixty went up at three o'clock, and then the captain changed the bowling at both ends, going on herself in place of Miss Frobisher, and trying Miss White at the other end. Mrs Coombes scored a 1 and a 2, and was then magnificently bowled and stumped by Miss White for 42. The retiring batswoman, who was loudly cheered, had been at the wickets for over three hours, during which time she had only given fourteen chances. Her chief hits were a 4 and three 3s. (7 for 65.) The end now soon came. Miss Fern was caught accidentally by Miss Waters for a useful 2, and two of the remaining batswomen were dismissed without scoring, the innings closing for 68, Miss Fulton carrying out her bat for a capital 1.

The Visitors had an up-hill battle to fight, 68 being the largest score yet made on this ground. The captain (Miss Milly Trenchard) went to the wickets first, accompanied by Miss Morley. The bowling was entrusted to Miss Fulton and Miss Tompkins (both slow under-

[49]

hand). The innings opened badly, the captain being bowled first ball by long-stop in returning the ball to the wicket-keeper. Miss White followed, and quickly lifted Miss Fulton to the off for 2. Two byes were recorded, and then Miss Morley broke her duck with a 1 into the hands of mid-wicket, who dropped it, and refused to stand there any longer. At 7 a high one from Miss Tompkins spreadeagled Miss White's wickets, and Miss Waters came in. This lady is the most brilliant batswoman on the Visitors' side, owing to her running powers, which enable her to score two for every other person's one. On this occasion she unfortunately lost her head. Missing the ball at her first try at it, she ran after it, and overtaking it near long-stop, propelled it as hard as she could. The ball went so far that it required four fielders flinging it as hard as they could to return it to the wicket-keeper. In the meantime Miss Waters had been running swiftly between the wickets, passing Miss Morley (who is a slow runner) repeatedly, and shouting out 'How's that?' in a triumphant voice every time she touched the block-hole. Mrs Coombes, the wicket-keeper, concealed the ball about her person until both batswomen were out of their ground, then stumped Miss Waters, and calling out 'Play' when Miss Morley's back was turned, quickly bowled that lady. Six runs had been made, but they cost two wickets (4 and 13). The next comers were Miss Ruby Willoughby and Mrs Maginn. The latter scored a leg-bye, and a wide, and Miss Willoughby added a brace of singles. Miss Maginn had a life from Miss Reid, who flung the ball to long-off instead of to the bowler, and her companion drew Miss Fulton to leg for 2, and lifted Miss Tompkins over the wicket-keeper's head for 3. 25 went up, and a change of bowling was tried, Miss Townley (lobs) going on *vice* Miss Tompkins. At 28 Mrs Maginn fell over her wickets, for which she was allowed 2. Immediately afterwards she was caught and run out (5 for 30).

Ten minutes was here allowed for conversation, and then play was resumed, Miss Willoughby having Miss Grainger for partner. These two ladies subjected Eastbourne to a rare piece of leather-hunting, and 40 went up after half-an-hour's play. At 31, 32, 34, 36 and 37 Miss Willoughby should have been stumped, and Miss Grainger was nearly caught at 32, 36, 38 and 39. Miss Freda Townley, one of the

[50]

fielders, added 2 to the in-side by making a mistake in fielding. On picking up the ball, instead of returning it to the bowler, she kept it in her hands and began to run as hard as she could between the wickets under the impression that by this means she was adding to her own score. When she had run twice from wicket to wicket the ball was taken from her, and two counted in favour of Miss Willoughby, who had also been running. Miss Grainger was bowled at 41, and Miss Metcalf, who took her place, fell to a twister from Miss Tompkins (seven for 41). The chances were now all against the visitors being able to stave off a defeat, and Mrs Salmond, the next comer, was told to play for a draw. The score slowly rose to 43, and then Miss Fern took the leather from Miss Tompkins. Her first over being a maiden, she was sent back to cover-point, and Mrs Hastings was tried with the ball. A 'rot' now set in; indeed it is not likely that had Mrs Hastings been tried earlier the Visitors would have remained at the wickets so long. This lady, like all good bowlers, has a method of her own. She runs half way up the pitch before delivering the ball, and then pretends to bowl. The bat-woman, seeing her arm moving, thinks she has bowled and strikes out at nothing. When the bat is in the air Mrs Hastings quickly flings the ball at the wicket with unfailing aim. Mrs Salmond and Miss Frobisher fell to her in two successive balls, and Miss Willoughby almost immediately afterwards, so that Mrs Hastings all but did the hat trick. The innings closed for 43, leaving Eastbourne easily victorious.

The victory was mainly due to the fine batting of Mrs Coombes, the only other batswoman who succeeded in getting into double figures being Miss Willoughby, who made 17 by superb cricket. There were those in the field who considered Miss Willoughby's form better than Mrs Coombes', her forward play being very fine, and her back drives to slip generally admired. None of the unseemly altercations that so often take place in men's matches spoilt this one, the only point on which there was any diversity of opinion being whether 43 is less than 68 by 19 or by 27. Appended are the scores:

EASTBOURNE

Miss Lucy Townley, b Miss Metcalf	4
Mrs Coombes, b and st Miss White	42
Miss Rogers, retired muddy	0
Miss Tower, b Miss Metcalf	3
Mrs Hastings, st Miss Waters, b Miss White	2
Miss Reid, st Mrs Salmond, b Miss White	0
Miss Tompkins, st Mrs Salmond, b Miss Metcalf	2
Miss Fern, c Miss Waters, lbw Miss Frobisher	2
Miss Fulton, not out	1
Miss Rhoda Townley, b Miss Metcalf	0
Miss G. Smithers, b Miss White	0
Extras	12
Total	68

VISITORS

Miss Nelly Trenchard (capt.), b Miss Reid	0
Miss Morley, b Mrs Coombes	1
Miss White, b Miss Tompkins	2
Miss Waters, st and c Mrs Coombes	6
Miss Ruby Willoughby, b Mrs Hastings	17
Mrs Maginn, c and run out Miss Rogers	4
Miss Frobisher, b Mrs Hastings	0
Miss Katie Metcalf, b Miss Tompkins	0
Mrs Salmond, b Mrs Hastings	0
Miss Lucy Wilson, not out	0
Miss Grainger, b Miss Tompkins	1
Extras	12
Total	43

Edinburgh Evening Dispatch, 17 August 1887

A CRICKETER EXPLAINS
(Strange Misfortunes on the Cricket Field)

This week we concluded our engagements for the present season. I
am not going to say what the name of our club is, but it begins with a
C, and our averages are to be published presently in the *Dispatch*. It is
this that induces me to explain in print why I have not this year come
up to expectation. Going home from the office yesterday I met our
club secretary on George IV Bridge, and he informed me that he was
drawing up a list of averages for publication. This annoyed me a good
deal, and I pointed out to him that it was not the right thing to do.
Why, I said, make our private amusements public property? He
chuckled at this in a way that made me hate him, and, said he, 'Why,
it was you who insisted at the beginning of the season that our
averages should be printed in the newspapers at the end of it.'

I detest a fellow who goes back upon what one said months ago,
and I told our secretary so. He grinned again.

'I guess,' he said, 'you thought at that time that you would come
out at the head of the averages instead of at the –?'

'So I would,' I interposed angrily, 'if it had not been for –'

'Been for what?'

'Why, for the circumstances.'

'What circumstances?'

I could not think of them at the moment, but here are the
circumstances now.

Our secretary was quite right in insinuating that when the season
began I was in hopes of having the best batting averages. My belief
was well grounded, for I am the best bat in the eleven, as they would
all admit if they did not have such a high opinion of their own batting
powers.

The opening match of the season was played on our own ground,
our opponents also being an Edinburgh club. I had ill-luck from the
first, for the other side won the toss, and owing to an accident I failed
to catch their captain in his second over. I am really a fine fielder, but
in this case the ball came to me so unexpectedly that I had no time to
get used to it. The sun, too, was in my eyes, and the ground being soft
I slipped. Nothing could be more obvious than that I missed the ball

[53]

by an accident, but for all that the spectators shouted out 'butter-fingers', and our captain sent me to field somewhere else. I was a little indignant, but 'never mind,' I said to myself, 'wait till my turn comes to bat.'

It was my first year in this club, and they had never seen me batting except when we were practising. I don't show well at practice, because there is no glory to be gained by it, but I told them that in matches I play carefully at first until I get a mastery over the bowling, after which I hit it all over the field. I was just the man they needed, so they arranged that I should go in second wicket down. H. and B. opened the batting for our side, and played very badly, the three first overs only resulting in one run. My fame as a batsman having spread among the spectators, I had a little crowd round me while B. and H. were in. I felt it my duty to criticise the batting severely.

'Well played, B,' someone cried, as B. slipped the ball for one.

'You are quite wrong,' I said. 'B. should have cut that for two or three at the least. It was a beautiful ball for cutting.'

I had a bat in my hand, and showed them how the ball should have been played.

'That was a good drive, at any rate,' someone said, as H. lifted the ball for two.

'H. did not catch the ball on the proper point of his bat,' I explained, 'or he would have driven it to the ropes. His forward play is clumsy.'

When the score had reached 15, H. was clean bowled.

'The ball twisted in off my pads,' he said, on returning to the pavilion.

I detest hearing a man excusing himself in this way, my own rule always being to admit a blunder if I make one.

'It was an easy ball to play,' I told him, 'if you had stepped out to it.'

W. was now in with B., and runs came slowly. I saw opportunity after opportunity missed: indeed, had I got these balls, I knew perfectly well that I would have subjected the fielders to a rare piece of leather-hunting.

'The play is tame beyond description,' I said.

'That is because the bowlers are dead on the wicket,' said H.

[54]

'I confess,' I said, 'that I see no reason for blocking because the bowling is straight. The proper way to treat these balls is to lift them over the bowler's head.'

'Now is your chance to do it, then,' said H., for while I spoke B. was caught at the wicket. The total was now 31.

As I walked to the wicket there was a cheer from the crowd, for they wanted lively play. I lifted my cap in acknowledgment, and took up my position. I had never felt in better form, and as the ball left the bowler's hand I made up my mind to send it towards the pavilion. When it was half way towards me I thought to myself, would it not be better to play a cautious game at first? This uncertainty was fatal, for before I could make up my mind the middle wicket was down.

'How's that?' cried the bowler, to whom I took an immediate dislike.

'Out,' replied the umpire, who was a most offensive fellow.

There would have been no use arguing the matter with them, so I returned to the pavilion. I did not want the cheers of the spectators; but still it struck me that their jeers following so soon after their applause showed how fickle and unreasoning they were. Our captain was just as bad, and said something about a duck's egg that I treated with silent contempt.

'You should have lifted that ball over the bowler's head,' said H.

'You are not the man to block a ball because it happens to be straight,' said B.

So they went on, as if, standing in the pavilion, they could possibly see how the ball should have been played. It is easy to brag in this way when you are watching the play from a distance. Brag of any kind, however, is detestable.

Our second match was also played in Edinburgh, though not on our own ground. This time, for a reason that I could never discover, our captain put me in sixth. It was a foolish thing to do, as I pointed out to him, for if I got well set, as would probably be the case, I would not have a chance of making a very big score before the tenth wicket fell.

'If you carry out your bat,' he said, 'I shall put you in fourth in the second innings.'

Unfortunately I did not carry out my bat. The very first ball I got I hit for 2, and the captain shouted out, 'Well hit, sir'. After that I got no balls for some time, the man who was in along with me getting them all. This was to be regretted for the sake of our club, for he blocked ball after ball that I could have sent away for 2 and 3. I was amazed to see him play so gingerly when the bowling was so weak.

At last my turn came again. The ball was breaking from the off when I drew it beautifully. I did not see where it went to, but the other batsman, B., shouted 'Run', and I ran.

'Another,' he cried, beginning to run again.

My idea was that I had hit the ball, and I thought I saw cover-point flinging it to the wicket-keeper.

'Go back,' I shouted to B.

'It's an easy run,' he panted, for being quicker sighted than I he knew that I had hit the ball to leg.

There was a yelling of advice from the pavilion, but I would not run, and the result was that B. was run out before he could get back to his wickets. With an unreasonableness that made me feel sorry for him, he put all the blame on my head, and came dancing up to me in a passion.

'You ass!' he cried.

I smiled.

'What do you mean by running me out in this way?' he growled, looking as if he could strike me.

'It was your own fault,' I said.

'Not a bit of it. There was abundance of time.'

'I thought I cut the ball to cover-point.'

'What! You thought you had hit to leg! Well, you are a curiosity in cricket.'

So he went off fuming, as men of his type do. The proper course in the circumstances, of course, would have been to admit good-naturedly that the fault was his own. But he is not enough of a gentleman to do that.

I had now scored 3 in all, and felt that I was beating the bowling. No cricketing reader requires to be told that there are occasions when a batsman feels that he is in magnificent form. Then his eye is quick, all nervousness has worn off, and he is in a condition for rapid scoring. Those were now my feelings, and I daresay the 'out' side could read them in my face. At all events, I saw their captain send one or two of them further away from the wickets. Either he was frightened that they were not safe in close proximity to me, or he thought there was a chance of a catch at the ropes.

The next ball I got I drove vigorously, but the bowler stopped it. If he had been in his proper place it would have passed him, but he was a restless fellow, who could not stand still. His next ball was a 'yorker', and I missed it. It struck my leg.

'How's that?' someone cried.

'Out,' said the umpire.

'Who is out?' I asked.

'You are,' said the wicket-keeper.

'Out! How can I be out?'

'Lbw,' said the umpire.

This was a little too much.

'Do you mean to say,' I said, 'that my leg is in front of the wicket? Good gracious man, come and look.'

'That won't do,' said the wicket-keeper.

'What won't do?'

'None of your blarney.'

'I insist,' I said, 'upon knowing what you mean.'

'Why, that is not where your leg was when the ball hit it.'

'I haven't moved it an inch.'

'You've moved it half a yard.'

'Next man,' shouted the umpire.

In the whole course of my cricketing experience I have known nothing more infamous. I can only conclude that they saw they would never get me out by fair means and so determined to dispose of me foully. The worst of it was that I got no sympathy from my own side. I wanted them to stop the match, but they said 'fudge'. When I insisted with the captain that my leg was not in front of the wickets, he said, 'That is what they all say when they are out lbw,' implying that I was trying to cheat. I, who pride myself on nothing so much as my honesty. I asked him fiercely if that was what he meant, and he replied that it was. This so disgusted me that I went away and sat by myself on the fence.

In the second innings I was given out caught by the wicket-keeper, though I never touched the ball. It is not my intention to describe my misfortunes step by step, for that would occupy too much space, and besides, one match was very like another. All through the season I never got a chance of showing what I could do, because just when I was settling down to a big score I was put out. The games on our own ground I did not do well in, because somehow I never feel in good form on our own ground, while on other grounds I cannot play well because I am not used to them. It was my miserable luck, too, always to get difficult balls to play when I went in. The other men on our side got balls I could have hit out of the grounds, but no such balls ever came to me. Just because I never made big scores, too, our captain argued that I was not a good player, and he took to putting me in last man. Three times I was put out lbw, most unfairly, twice I was run out entirely through the fault of others, and I was caught four times by fielders who were standing in the wrong place. The luck, indeed, has been hopeless against me all through the year, and I have never had a chance of distinguishing myself.

Edinburgh Evening Dispatch, 1 September 1888

GRAND CRICKET MATCH
'Celebrities at Home' v. Stoke-in-the-Ditch

A cricket match, not without its amusing features, was played on Saturday last at a little Surrey village within five or six miles of Dorking. Here it may be called Stoke-in-the-Ditch. The home team was a local eleven, captained by the innkeeper, and the visitors were all from London. They called themselves the 'Celebrities at Home', because the original idea was to get up an eleven from persons who had figured under that heading in the *World*, and, I believe, seven of the team really had this qualification. The whole affair was a joke, got up by a barrister (and member of Parliament), who has been employed in the Parnell Commission, and is something of a humorist. The scene of the match was the village I call Stoke-in-the-Hole, because it is a favourite resort of artists, two of whom were in the team.

It would be unfair to give the names of the celebrities, as several of them stipulated for secrecy, and all played under assumed names. Besides the two artists and the barrister, who captained the eleven,

[58]

there played two members of Parliament, a dramatist, two men of letters, two journalists, and a scientist. The majority had not played cricket for a score of years, and, according to the captain, one was all along under the impression that he was playing at football. Everything divulged by this captain at the inn dinner, which followed the match, is perhaps not to be taken literally, for he was in high spirits; but his remarks were, no doubt, founded on fact. According to him, the scientist got a book of cricket rules for private digestion, and for some days before the match practised in his study with one of the MP's, the bat being a paper-knife, the wickets as ash-tray, and the ball a roll of newspaper. 'I called one evening,' said the barrister, 'and when I got as far as the hall I heard shouts of "Play!" followed by a noise as of someone falling over a chair. "I think my husband has gone mad," the lady of the house said to me, and upon my word I thought so too when I entered the study. The table had been pushed to the wall, with several chairs on the top of it, but the strangest spectacle of all was presented by the two cricketers. They were sitting, one on a chair, the other on the floor, glaring sulkily at each other, and I discovered that there was a difference of opinion as to whether our friend – had caught – out. The former had caught the ball fairly he said, while the batsman insisted that he had merely plucked it out of the curtain into which it had been hit. Had I not managed to calm them, I don't know what would have happened. There would probably have been a fight for the bat.' Were I to give the names of the two gentlemen, who are both past middle age, this picture would seem as grotesque to the reader as it did to the party at the inn.

Cards were printed and distributed on the field, containing interesting information about the Celebrities Eleven. These were drawn up, it is understood, by the barrister, who, mercifully, only gave the assumed names of his teams. The following is the card:

'Celebrities at Home'
Cricket Eleven,
1889.

Sir Walter Raleigh (captain) – A brilliant bat when well set; has a difficulty in getting set.

Robert Elsmere – Good all round man. Played consistently well last season. Smart in the field.

Lord Fauntleroy – Good change bowler. Generally goes in last man, and has been known to carry out his bat.

Richard Turpin (prof.) – A dangerous man anywhere.

Peter Boulanger – Said to be good in the field, but never tested so far.

John Ward – A terrific punisher of loose bowling.

Alan Quatermain – Captained a team in Africa, and scored heavily against the Zulus. Has been in poor form of late.

Silas Marner – A deadly bowler on a hard wicket.

Billy Sykes (prof.) – A pretty player, but very unlucky.

Alan Breck – Would be a fine player if he had more confidence in himself.

Gabriel Oak – Plays for the county of Wessex. Unfortunate with the bat and ball, and no use in the field, but otherwise a safe man.

The majority of the team travelled to Stoke-in-the-Ditch on Saturday forenoon, but the barrister went down the night before. He met them at the station. One of their difficulties was that there was not a man among them who had courage to carry a cricket bat through the London streets or even to conceal it in a hansom. The bats, etc., were therefore sent down to Stoke-in-the-Ditch direct from the shop where they were purchased. They were lying at Stoke-in-the-Ditch station when the train arrived, and here they had to be shouldered. The bold captain took one, but only with such difficulty could any one be persuaded to touch the others. Two players hid themselves to the waiting-room, thinking to steal un-ostentatiously to the cricket ground behind the others, but they were captured, and the eleven marched off in a body. Never, perhaps, did eleven eminent men look so sheepish. The whole village turned out to greet them, for which welcome the barrister was responsible. He had distributed his cards among the natives, who took them seriously, believed that a renowned cricket eleven had honoured them with a visit, and had a particular interest in 'Lord Fauntleroy', whom the captain kindly pointed out. This jocular man had gone to the expense of having great yellow posters stuck up all over the village, and the visitors had no sooner past one saying in letters half a foot long –

ROBERT ELSMERE IS IN GRAND FORM

than they had to face another announcing that

SILAS MARNER WILL POSITIVELY PLAY.

The local team, of course, knew more of the real constitution of their antagonists, but the public which assembled on the ground to the number of nearly a hundred, looked forward to magnificent play, and wondered at the daring of their local team in standing up before such men.

The Celebrities won the toss, and immediately decided to send their opponents in, their argument being that they themselves would look less idiotic in the field than at the bat. By this time the captain was probably the only man in the eleven who did not wish that he was back in London. He had some trouble in setting his field, partly because he did not know the technical terms, and partly because it had got out among them that long-on was the safest place to stand at. No less than seven men insisted on standing long-on, and harmony was only restored by the captain's promise that they should field there time about. Soon after the match started a disturbance was raised by the dramatist, who had never played cricket in his life, and had consented to stand at point on the understanding that his duties would be slight and pleasant. The barrister's third and fourth balls hit him, however, severely in the stomach, and in the next over he was knocked over by the batsman. After this he threatened to leave the field unless he was allowed to be long-on. As the ball had been driven for four and lifted for five and cut repeatedly for threes, it was now decided that the 'out' field was the place to send maimed men to, and thus it came about that soon there was no point, no wicket-keeper, and no mid-wicket. The slip stood afar off, and had too much caution to touch the ball until it stopped.

It is not necessary to tell how the villagers 'mastered the bowling', though did space allow it would only be fair to describe the sensation

[61]

when Alan Breck bowled one man, and Peter Boulanger caught another out. Boulanger's catch was the merest accident, but he grew very proud of it when he realised slowly that he really had caught the ball.

The home team made 100 for four wickets, and then, taking advantage of the new rules, declared their innings at an end. Before the match began the Celebrities had crowded round their captain, each one insisting that he should go in last man. The captain pointed out that they could not all go in last man, and then they said that at least none of them would go in first man, which was quite as awkward. But their practice in the field made them bold. They had watched the batsmen until they felt convinced that batting was much easier than fielding, and now Billy Sykes, Lord Fauntleroy, Gabriel Oak, and John Ward all offered to open the innings. Eventually Sir Walter Raleigh and John Ward put on the pads and advanced to the fray. To the admiration and envy of his side, John Ward (a journalist) stepped out boldly to a leg ball and cut it past point. For this he scored two amid tremendous applause. This was the biggest hit made by the Celebrities that day, though Ward was not the heaviest scorer, Richard Turpin succeeding, by brilliant and careful batting, in amassing three. The following is the complete score:

John Ward, b Gray	2
Sir Walter Raleigh, b do	0
Gabriel Oak, b do	0
Lord Fauntleroy, b Mainwaring	1
Alan Breck, b do	0
Silas Marner, b Gray	0
Richard Turpin (prof.), b Mainwaring	3
Billy Sykes (prof.), b Mainwaring	0
Alan Quatermain, b do	0
Peter Boulanger, b Gray	0
Robert Elsmere, b do	0
Byes	7
Total	13

The one fear that distressed the Celebrities was that Mainwaring or Gray might be a swift bowler, but as it turned out, this swift bowling proved very useful, for it gave them no less than seven byes. The dinner in the inn was a very animated affair, and the general feeling was that the eleven had been beaten but not disgraced. The voices heard oftenest above the din were those of Boulanger, explaining again and again how he caught that man out, and John Ward's analysis of his sensations when he hit Mainwaring for 2. I heard yesterday that a society paper is very anxious to get the real names of the eleven.

Edinburgh Evening Dispatch, 11 May 1889

URCHINS AT PLAY
(a Parallel)

My window is where four merry streets meet, and here, amid the clatter of cabs, carts, and lorries, a cricket club chooses to cast its stumps. The bat has been kicked out of a paling, the ball may be of india-rubber or only a cap tied round with twine, and the wickets are the jackets of the players who have any. The club comes and goes. When I leave my window to look for a match, the square may be deserted; I return, to find the field set and the game going boisterously. Suddenly there is the tramp of a guardian of the peace, when the cricketers with their paraphernalia seem to sink into the earth. The bluecoat rounds a corner, and, behold! the wickets are again pitched.

Within ten minutes of my rooms is a public park, to which go little boys, who call these ragmuffins cads. They are attired either in sailor suits, with the name of the ship which they sail in papa's pond on their straw hats, or in velveteens which do not quite reach the knee. In age they are much as the ragamuffins, but otherwise how different. They, too, play cricket, only they have real bats and wickets, which they carry to the park, or, when they are tired, give to the lady who accompanies them to carry. There is always a lady with them, sometimes their mother, but usually the person called a nursery governess. She has sunk her individuality for ten pounds a year, and

[63]

pretends to be mightily interested in her charges. When they hit her with the bat, she sees that it is a joke, and accepts it as such. If they ask her the same question ten times running, she answers it with apparent interest. If they laugh, she too laughs; and if they cry because one of the ragamuffins in passing knocked their dainty hats off, she coaxes them into being brave again. She joins them in their games with artificial relish, and there is praise for them every time they hit the ball. They become sulky if she does not praise them, and when they kick the wickets she puts it down to high spirits. The last time I was in the park a terrible disaster happened to these graceful little gentlemen. After the wickets were pitched they discovered that they had forgotten the ball. Of course they blamed the governess, and equally of course, there was no cricket that day. Despite their pretty bats, and sailor suits, and beautiful golden curls, they had to go home without a game. The ragamuffins would have guyed them. These ragged urchins are never in want of a ball. If they don't have one, they make one in no time. They are never at a loss. When they kick the wickets, as they do at times, there is no governess to pet them, but, instead, the owners of the wickets punch their heads. If they hit the ball, no one tells them they are clever; but if the ball hits the wickets, there are half-a-dozen to call them asses. If they fling the ball away in spleen, the cap is snatched from their head, and then the club has a ball again. They have a vulgar way of putting their fingers to their nose, and are adepts at chaffing cabbies. If the cabby catches them on the legs with his whip, their comrades laugh joyfully; and if the game is a little slow, they dance in a puddle. When they fall in the gutters there is no weeping; a little mud more or less on their breeches being a trifle; and when they smash a window they give a cheer, and bolt. The ragamuffins are more interesting than the velveteens.

I used to think that the cricketers who play before my window tossed for first innings. I saw them apparently tossing a penny, and then looking to see whether it fell head or tail. This 'business', as they would say at the theatres, seemed to divert them mightily, but I have since discovered that it is all sport. The idea of any one of them having a penny, or even a halfpenny, in his possession without immediately rushing off to turn it into toffy is too funny for them,

Barrie's powers of persuasion never more apparent. Sylvia Llewelyn Davies, mother of J.M.B's 'adopted' boys, attempting classic batting poses, possibly in the garden at Egerton House, Berkhamsted, *circa* 1905, or perhaps earlier at 31 Kensington Park Gardens.

J. M. Barrie.
133 Gloucester Road
London S.W.

Allahakbarries

CRICKET CLUB.

CRICKET

SCORING BOOK

Season

The _____ Cricket Club v. the _____ Cricket Club.

Match Played at _____ on _____ 18___

Innings of _Allahakbarries_ Result _____

	BATSMAN.	RUNS SCORED.	HOW OUT.	BOWLER.	TOTAL.
1	S. J. _____	41.3.41.2.31.	b w	Osborne	9
2	A. Dixon		b b	Saunders	22
3	H. J. Ford	13.2./3.1.1.3.1.7.2.4.3.11.	bowled	Saunders	32
4	H. Pritchard	3.2.4.1.3.2.1.2.3.3.	bowled	Ernest Brown	23
5	H. Meredith		lbw	Saunders	0
6	B. Partridge	13.	stumps	Saunders	4
7	S. Pauling	3.4.13.1.3.2.1.9.3.2.1.1.	bowled	Saunders	34
8	J. M. Barrie	3.	bowled	Saunders	31
9	A. E. W. Mason		not out	Saunders	0
10	E. V. Lucas	2.1.	bowled	b 30	4
11	_____		bowled	bowled	7
	UMPIRE	Byes 1.3.1.			
		Leg Byes			
		Wide Balls 1			
		No Balls			
				Total of Innings.	134

Runs at the fall of each Wicket	1	2	3	4	5	6	7	8	9	10
	5	30	87	87	87	101	119			

BOWLING ANALYSIS.

BOWLER.	RUNS FROM EACH OVER.	Overs	Maidens	Wides	No Balls	Runs	Wickets

Pages from an Allahakbarries' scorebook which noted their stirring deeds from 1899 to 1903.

The Allahakbarries at Black Lake near Farnham in 1905, where games were played on the south lawn of the Barrie's country retreat. *Back row*, L to R: Maurice Hewlett, J.M.B., Harry Graham, E.V. Lucas. *Front row*, L to R: H.J. Ford, A.E.W. Mason, Charles Tennyson, Charles Turley Smith. The child in the middle is Michael Llewelyn Davies. The photograph was taken by Edgar Horne.

The wash-house at the back of Barrie's birthplace in the Tenements, Kirriemuir. It was the inspiration for Wendy's little home in *Peter Pan*.

George Llewelyn Davies taking a stunning catch to dismiss G. Wilson for Eton against Harrow at Lord's in 1912 in front of a crowd of 15,000. The chance arrived on his 'right' side; he was a left-handed batsman. Barrie's 'boy' scored 59 in Eton's first innings after surviving a stumping chance when only 1 and also bowled Harrow's top-scoring captain who had made 137.

The Allahakbarries taking a final call before World War I intervened. On this occasion, in July 1913, they pitted their skill against E.V. Lucas's XI at Downe House. *Back row*, L to R: George (with such a name who needs another?), Thomas Gilmour, Will Meredith, George Meredith jnr., Denis Mackail, Harry Graham, Dr. Goffe. *Centre row*, L to R: A.A. Milne, Maurice Hewlett, J.M.B., George Morrow, E.V. Lucas, Walter Frith. *Front row*,

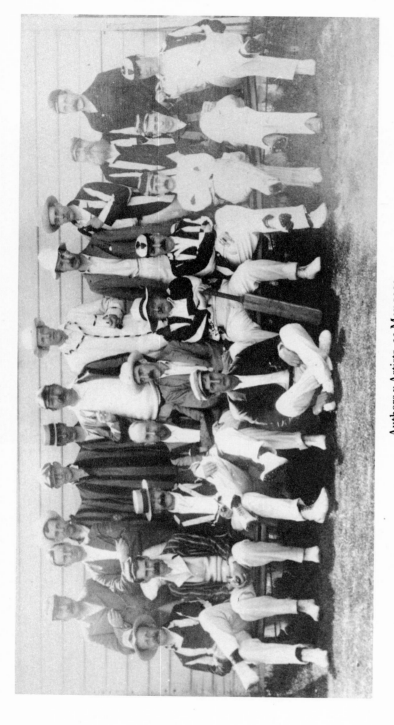

Authors v Artists, 22 May 1903.

Back row, L to R: E.W. Hornung, E.V. Lucas, P.G. Wodehouse, J.C. Smith, G. Charne, Sir A. Conan Doyle, Hesketh Prichard, L.D. Luard, C.M.Q Orchardson, L.C. Nightingale, A. Kinross. *Front row*, L to R: C. Gascoyne, Shan F. Bullock, G. Hillyard Swinstead, Reginald Blomfield, Hon. W.J. James, E.A. Abbey, A. Chevalier Taylor, J.M. Barrie, G.C. Ives, G. Spencer Watson, (sitting on ground) A.E.W. Mason.

Barrie's birthplace: Lilybank in the Tenements, Kirriemuir.

and as a grand joke they go many times a day through the form of tossing a penny. It is all done in dumb show, but the humour of the action never palls. Very possibly the velveteens are not certain whether they have a penny in their pockets till they feel, and their life is such that if they have one they can be happy without at once spending it. The ragamuffin gets more fun out of not having a penny than they out of having one. Sometimes I have flung a penny to the cricketers from my window. The first time it created a sensation. One of the most diminutive of them saw it fall, and having grasped it, could do nothing for a time but shriek, 'I've got a penny. I've got a penny!' The others disbelieved him at first, but he became a hero as soon as they had seen the penny with their own eyes. It was interesting to watch the centre of attraction proud to show that it was a genuine penny and at the same time fearful that they would take it from him. I signed from the window that it was for them all, but they were evidently afraid I was wanting the penny back, for they up with the wickets, and fled from the locality. Half an hour afterwards I came upon them sitting in a row on a door-step solemnly munching apples.

The velveteens are not even afraid of the policeman, and stroll by him as if he were nothing to them. Some may say that this shows a clean conscience, but I don't admire it. The birthright of boys is to run from the policeman, whom they look upon as their natural enemy. The ragamuffins enjoy this right to the full. It is difficult to say whether they really believe that policemen wander about the streets looking for them, but they certainly have always an eye looking for the policeman. When they are what they consider a safe distance from him they sometimes shout sarcasm at his helmet, and even refer wittingly to the cook. Thus they don't regard him with the awe of the boy who asked his mother if 'nobody was quite good – what, not even the policeman?' One would like to know whether they think the policeman is paid to chase them, or whether they regard him as a man of means, who does it for his own entertainment or the country's good. When they realise that it is such as they who pay for policemen, they will get a shock.

Such a terror to the ragamuffin-cricketers is the policeman that they think adults also tremble at his approach. I have seen them pretend that the policeman was on their side, a magnificently audacious argument. This was one day when they were playing with a real india-rubber ball. Several times it went down our area. Then I discovered that ragamuffins have a way that is their own of descending areas. There were the gate and the stairs, which offered the easiest and more customary method of descent, but these they ignored. Their method of getting downstairs was to climb the railings, on the top of which they sat curled up, like hedgehogs spiked there and left as a warning to other ragamuffins. Then they dropped into the area, seized the ball, and rushed up the stairs, a servant at their heels with a besom. At last, however, the much suffering servant was too much for them. She pounced on the ball and confiscated it. They sat down on the railings, balancing themselves amazingly, for a fall backwards would have meant dislocation, and there they held a council of war. They tried several ways of getting the ball back, such as ringing for it and shouting opprobrious epithets at the servant, and when these failed they actually had the audacity to threaten her with the policeman. I heard them from my open window gravely agreeing that the servant had been guilty of theft, and one of them, who seemed well up in the law, said that the policeman could give her seven days. The general impression apparently was that the policeman's decision in these matters was final, and that he sentenced all criminals as well as took them in custody. He marches his captives to prison, and as he flings them into a cell, tells the warder to 'give this one seven days' and 'that one a fortnight'. The servant could not have failed to hear these threats, but she defied her foes, even when the one who was up in the law expressed his intention of going for the policeman at once. The ragamuffins were very stern and grave now. Evidently they felt that they had a sure case. On ordinary occasions they are more or less larky, but this time they really seemed in earnest. The ringleader got off the railing, and was actually on his way to bring the policeman, when in a momentary stillness there was heard the tramp, tramp of the man of the law. The ragamuffins looked at each other. Then as one boy they slipped from the railing and stole away.

Sometimes the policeman does get hold of one, and then you see how hardy the ragamuffin is. The great lumbering blue-coated fiend is the one person in the world whom he really fears, yet is he not craven. Making the best of things, though his heart is in his mouth, he defies the policeman. The latter having him by the neck probably wishes he had not, for he does not know what to do with him. He can only shake him, and then let him go. Now is the ragamuffin's chance. He refuses to go, he threatens the policeman's head with stones, while his comrades stand afar off and cheer lustily. Only when the ragamuffin has shuffled some yards away and sees the policeman about to make another rush at him, does he remember how glorious a thing is freedom. Then, turning tail, he vanishes down a side street. I never saw velveteens in the hands of the police, and perhaps it is libellous to conceive him in such a position. But suppose him laid violent hands on by mistake, the chances are that he would whimper until the governess came to his rescue. Velveteens may be the nicer boy, but the ragamuffin is to my mind the more interesting, and by and by he may become the better man of the two.

Edinburgh Evening Dispatch, 12 June 1889

THE OXFORD AND CAMBRIDGE MATCH
(A Picnic at Lord's)

One of the things which must strike visitors to London is that the majority of the 'buses run to public-houses. Taverns are the London landmarks. If you are bound for Highgate, you 'bus to the Archway Tavern or the Boston; if for Whiteley's, to the Royal Oak; if for Islington, to the Angel. At this moment, however, there is a rival in the field, for a great many 'buses, legitimate and 'pirates', show the single word 'Lord's'. In the neighbourhood of Lord's itself – indeed, all through St John's Wood – every road swarms with drags, hansoms, vehicles of every kind, and sweltering humanity, making for the cricket match or returning from it. At the most fashionable hour of the day the crush of conveyances is such that if a policeman loses his head for a moment, and so allows the road to get blocked, traffic is stopped for ten minutes all along the apparently endless line. To cross the road at such a time on one's feet is to be a Londoner, or rash to the point of folly. There is a story of some one from the

country who got to St John's Wood by train, after which two
minutes' walk brought him to within twenty yards of the entrance to
Lord's. Unfortunately he was on the wrong side of the road, and he
could not summon up courage to dive into the crowd of vehicles.
Finally he took a hansom, which was nearly half an hour in bringing
him to the gate, for it had to take up its position at the tail of the line of
carriages, and from there crawl along a yard at a time.

So far as fashion is concerned there is not much to choose between
the University match and that engaged in by Eton and Harrow.
There is only one event of the London season that is gayer – namely,
the Henley regatta – which does not, indeed, draw a more fashionable assemblage, but is made specially remarkable by the extraordinary show of houseboats. On the river Londoners go in for much
more brightly-coloured garments than anywhere else, and there
alone do the men vie in smart costumes with the women. Lord's at
present, however, is in more colours than are known to the rainbow,
and, if more carriages have been seen in some former years, the
weather was never more benignant. The scene can, perhaps, best be
compared to a theatre. It is, indeed, an open-air theatre on a
enormous scale, with 'stalls', 'boxes', and 'dress circle' for society,
and a mighty pit for the crowd. The boxes differ in no material
respect from those at the Lyceum, and they and the stalls are full of
fair ladies and more or less brave men. The carriages may be called
the private boxes, which the cream of fashion bring with them; and
here and there they contain a lady who casts an occasional glance at
the match. When you hear applause from the boxes, however, the
chances are that it is not an award of merit for a good cut to the ropes,
but for Lord Algernon's skilful way of drawing a champagne cork.
Hundreds of picnics are being held in those boxes, and hundreds
more at houses that hoop Lord's round, for it is good form for the
tenants of these to invite their friends to chicken and champagne
when Oxford is playing Cambridge.

Every one knows the story of the first wrangler who thought
it prudent not to go up to London until the excitement in the
Metropolis about his triumph had subsided. Had he been in the
University's first eleven he would have known better than to fancy
himself the talk of London, for the cricketers at Lord's must be well

[68]

aware that their match is only an opportunity for the picnic, and the cause of it. True, the fashionable rabble wear the colours of the Universities, but there their interest in the contest ends; and if they have no brothers or cousins in one of the elevens, they wear the colour that suits them best. It is her complexion that makes the pretty girl in yellow a 'dark blue'. The Eton and Harrow boys have not, however, realised that London does not gather in its thousands at Lord's to see them play, and it is pleasant to observe their airs.

'I know Linton who made 44 not out,' says an Eton boy to his friends, in the tone of one who boasted personal friendship with Julius Caesar.

'Be a good girl,' says lordly little Harrow to his sister, who is engaged to Lord Thomas Noddy, 'and I'll perhaps get our captain to shake hands with you.'

But the grandest sight during the Eton and Harrow match is when Linton who made 44 takes a walk round. No victorious General entering Rome in triumph could strut more magnificently, or gather a more loyal crowd of worshippers. Linton allows one friend from Eton to carry his coat, and links his arms within those of two others who beam in his reflected glory. While he prances along, explaining that Harrow would never have bowled him though he had been at the wickets for a week, those in his vicinity listen with wide-open mouths, and others run in front, pointing him out to the public, and clearing a way for him through the crowd.

At the Oxford and Cambridge match a vast number of men, mostly young, are engaged, it is true, explaining the game of cricket to fair companions.

'You see, that fellow who bowls is called the bowler.'

'How interesting! And does he hurl the ball for the one with the bat to strike?'

'Why, yes, but –'

'Oh; and then when the ball hits the bat does that count one to the bowler?'

'No; on the contrary, if the batsman hits it and runs one, that counts one to him.'

'But I thought the bowler's aim was to hit the bat, and the batsman's to prevent his doing so?'

[69]

'No, no; the bowler wants to hit the wickets.'

'Oh; then, why does the batsman not stand further away from them, so as to give him a better chance?'

'Why, the whole idea of the game is that the one should try and foil the other.'

'Oh, I quite understand now, but is not that dreadfully selfish?'

We come to rest in the vicinity of some other box, where a patient gentleman is telling a lady with large eyes (that serve her better than intellect) all about it.

'Do you know, Lord Henry, who the cricketer is standing so far away from the others?'

'I forget his name, Miss Alice; but he is standing long-on.'

'I can't take my eyes off him.'

Happy man! but I admit he fields superbly.

'I do wonder why he stands so far away from the others. See, he is quite close to the ropes.'

'Oh, he stands there because he is long-on. He is in what is called the long field.'

'I wonder who she is.'

'Who?'

'The attraction.'

'Why, what do you mean?'

'Oh, he would never stand so far away from the others unless there were some attraction. But he is going away now.'

'He is only changing his place at the end of the over.'

'Ah, I feel sure he only does that to vex her.' (An over is bowled, and the field again changes.)

'See,' says Miss Alice, triumphantly, 'here he comes again. He can't stay away from her any time.'

'Look at that cricketer with the bat,' says a third lady; 'why is he going away?'

'He is out.'

'But I thought you said he was in?'

'Well, he was in a moment ago, but he is out now. Woods took his wicket.'

'I'm so sorry. Then does Mr Woods get the wicket to keep, or do they play for it again next year?'

[70]

We leave the cavalier explaining, and pass on.

'I do call that a handsome fellow,' says a lady, looking at a batsman who had just come in. 'I feel sure he will win.'

'But one man doesn't win. It is a whole side that wins.'

'Well, I hope his side will win. Which side is it?'

'Oxford.'

'And I am for Cambridge, am I not? Why does Cambridge not run?'

'Oh, it isn't their time yet.'

'I feel sure Oxford will win.'

'Oh, you are wrong there. The batting is all in Cambridge's favour.'

'But Oxford have made so many runs.'

'No, they have done very badly. Why, they have six or seven wickets down for eighty.'

'Still, that is so much better than Cambridge. You told me they had not made any yet. How dreadfully humiliating if they don't make any all through this match!'

'But you misunderstand. Cambridge hasn't had an innings yet.'

'Yes, I know, but surely they might have made a few by this time. Oh!'

The exclamation was caused by the 'handsome fellow' spooning the ball high into coverpoint's hands.

'I told you he would win!' exclaimed the lady. 'See how the people are cheering him.'

'It is not he they are cheering, but the man who caught him. He is out.'

'Poor fellow!'

'I don't mean that the man who caught him is out, but the man you call so handsome.'

'Oh, what a shame; but how can he be out when he hit the ball so well? I am sure it was the highest hit that has been made today.'

'It was too high. You see the high balls are generally caught. Good play is to send the ball skimming along the turf.'

'Do you think so? I don't think so at all. It must be much more difficult to hit them high. They won't insist on his being out, will they?'

'Yes, of course. Don't you see him almost at the pavilion by this time?'

'And he looks so crestfallen. I think it such a shame not to give him another try. He is so handsome.'

There is a confusion of ideas, too, about the umpires.

'The Professors must be tired standing there all day,' says a lady.

'I don't see any of them.'

'Oh yes, there they are. Those two men in the white jackets and little hats.'

'No, no, those are the umpires.'

'Well, I understood that they were Professors. I am sure some one told me so.'

So it goes on year after year, and the intelligent foreigner who comes over to see this great country in ten days is impressed by nothing more than the interest English ladies take in cricket. He tells his friends that the interest is at fever point on the day of the Oxford and Cambridge match, and that the ladies are such hot partisans that they can't leave the field until the drawing of stumps. So they bring their luncheon with them. That they bring their luncheon is perfectly true; indeed, the intelligent foreigner would do a service could he calculate how many thousands of pounds are spent yearly on food, drink, and clothing for the Inter-University match.

Edinburgh Evening Dispatch, 3 July 1889

[4]

LOOSE CONNECTIONS

B<small>Y</small> the end of the 1880s, Barrie had consolidated his position as a
writer of distinction; the phenomenal rate of his literary outpourings
included five published books and shortly he was to make ventures as
a dramatist on the London stage. Cricket was not forgotten – both watching
it, more often than not at Lord's, in the company of a friend from his
Nottingham days, T. L. Gilmour, and also referring to the game in his
work. An instance of this is to be found in a novelette of some twenty
thousand words entitled *A Superfluous Man*, which appeared monthly
throughout 1889 in a periodical called *Young Man*.

A transparent autobiographical note is sounded (arguably, less shielded
in Barrie's work than any other writer's) in the figure of Dan Moore, who
leaves Ballyhewan for London and of whom 'it had better be admitted at
once that he would have preferred seeing the Australian cricketers to
spending an evening at Exeter Hall'.

A Superfluous Man is a variation on the theme of *When a Man's Single*, a
tale of literary life (published in 1888) in which the character of Rob Angus
is another portrayal of the experiences of the young Barrie. Noble Simms,
the editor, advises Rob that when anything remarkable happens in London
he should immediately write an article on the times the same thing has
happened before. 'Don't neglect eclipses,' he says, 'nor heavy scoring at
cricket matches any more than what look like signs of the times, and always
try to be first in the field.'

Another cricketing quote is to be found in the chapter 'Scorn of Scorns'
when the school captain, Greybrooke, in conversation with Nell Meredith
and wishing to show how angry and involved he was on her behalf (Miss
Meredith's novel had been criticized in the local *Mirror*), 'expressed
involuntarily a wish that Nell could see him punishing loose bowling'.

Earlier in the book, before Nell Meredith had met her ardent admirer, she spoke disparagingly of him in response to remarks made by the hero-worshipping Will Abinger. Adopting an air of superiority given only to the young, Abinger declares: 'He made a hundred and three against Rugby, and was only bowled off his pads'. Ultimately though, Greybrooke fails the sternest test, 'he found that he had to give up either Nell or a cricket match, and so Nell was reluctantly dropped'.

Elsewhere we read: 'Abinger discovered that the baronet [Sir Clement Dowton, a famous explorer] did not know what l.b.w. meant.' He 'could not, nevertheless, despise a man who had shot lions, but he never had quite the same respect for the king of beasts again'.

Barrie was adept at weaving a thread from one piece of writing into a tapestry for another. This is immediately obvious in the setting for much of *Walker, London*, which recalls the houseboat incident in *When a Man's Single*. *Walker, London*, Barrie's first really ambitious work for the theatre, was produced at Toole's Theatre (where later stood Charing Cross Hospital) and takes as its scenario the Thames, near Maidenhead. J. L. Toole himself was in the cast as the humble hairdresser, Jasper Phipps, and was joined by Seymour Hicks, Irene Vanbrugh and Barrie's future wife Mary Ansell, whom he insisted be given a part after she had been recommended by his cricketing friend, Jerome K. Jerome.

Cecil Ramsey played the boy's role called W.G. 'because he likes to fancy that he is a reincarnation of W. G. Grace, England's great nineteenth-century cricketer', and Barrie's instinctive identification with the mind of a boy is clearly perceptible. 'I would rather take three wickets in an over than be Shakespeare and Homer and all those swells put together.'

There are many references to the game:

NANNY (Mary Ansell): You call yourself W.G. because you think you are a great cricketer and I can bowl you myself.

W.G.: You bowl me! Oh, that time – because my foot slipped . . .

NANNY: And W.G., you needn't expect me to play in the cricket match on Saturday if you say I bowled unfairly.

W.G. (alarmed): Don't say you won't play, Cousin Nanny. I say, I'm not angry with you for kissing me; I know girls can't help it. And look here, read that letter I've been writing to Daly Major, and you'll see how I crack up your leg hits.

NANNY (reading a letter written by W.G.): 'There is another girl on board, my cousin Nanny, and we are to have a cricket match next

Saturday in the village, men versus women. Nanny is good at high leg ones but I can always bowl her with a daisy cutter.' He can't! . . . Ah, Bell. Here is something about Mr Upjohn. 'Who do you think is staying at the inn? One of the greatest men of the day, namely Kit Upjohn who made 121 for Middlesex against Notts, and even then was only bowled off his pads [never waste a good line] . . . and then he offers me a cane-handled bat if I can run the mile in six minutes.'

W.G. (talking to Bell Golightly BA, played by Irene Vanbrugh): Great Balbus girl, why he made 121 against Notts. I say, I wonder what he saw in you? You are sure he wanted you? (Bell slaps his face and jumps into a punt.)

Act II. Stage direction: W.G. is practising cricket, the ball being suspended on a rope, hanging from a sort of crane.

W.G.: Well, don't forget any of you that we start for the cricket match, men versus girls, in half an hour . . . (W.G. tries to balance bat on his nose.)

ANDREW MCPHAIL (Seymour Hicks) (on receiving a telegram): I've passed! I've passed! Great Scott! I've passed! (Falls hysterically into chair and telegram drops on deck. They shake his hand, he jumps up.) I've passed! (Runs to top of ladder.) Colonel Neil, I've passed! (Runs down ladder.) Ben, I've passed! (Rushes through saloon.) Penny, I've passed! (Goes into bedroom, dances wildly Highland fling for a moment, and into cabin, and then pulls down blind.)

MRS GOLIGHTLY (Ettie Liston): He is off his head. (Sits down and knits.)

BELL: About a common little medical degree. (Sits and reads.)

W.G.: I hope this won't spoil his form for the cricket match.

W.G. (on deck): You girls, isn't it time you were dressing for the cricket match?

BELL: I am dressed, *simplex munditiis.*

[75]

MRS GOLIGHTLY (on bank): Colonel, please tell W.G. that I want him to help me to wind this wool.

W.G. (looking down from deck): Can't, Mater, it would tire me for the match.

W.G. (at top of ladder): We start in five minutes remember, Bell.

W.G.: Hi, everybody – time to start.

JASPER: A moment, W.G. Run and play. (Turning to Bell) Bell, I love you.

ANDREW: But I am not coming with you. It wouldn't be professional to play cricket, and a physician must attend to medical etiquette.

NANNY: Do come!

MRS GOLIGHTLY: Do!

ANDREW: No.

JASPER: Come, though you don't play. There may be accidents, and a leg to set, or some stumps to draw.

W.G.: I say, Upjohn, what a pity you didn't come back in time for the match! The men played with broomsticks, you know, but I was in tremendous form. I lifted Nanny twice clear over the pavilion!

KIT UPJOHN (C. M. Lowne): We are engaged, W.G. – congratulate me!

W.G. (disgusted): Engaged. Oh hang it, you'll be no more use for anything!

JASPER (disappointed suitor – meekly): Is that you W.G.?

W.G.: If you are going out on the river, I'll come with you!

JASPER: No, W.G., I – I – am going away!

W.G.: Why? Because you were bowled for a duck's egg?

Walker, London ran for 511 performances from 25 February 1892. The farce was a great success commercially for Toole, who had bought all rights for £250. Barrie, however, retained very few fond memories for what he described as 'an early indiscretion'. In fact, when he learned, a few years before his death, that a management was eager to turn it into a musical comedy, he threatened legal action. In Barrie's mind, perhaps *Walker, London* was too closely associated with the period in which he began his liaison with Mary Ansell. It is a truism that the march of time sometimes passes too close to paths that led only to despair.

THE ALLAHAKBARRIES

THE story of how Barrie's colourful cricket team was formed has been recounted many times – not that it ever palls – not least by the great man himself, in speeches, at social events and, of course, in *The Greenwood Hat*.

Cricket had been my joy since I first saw it played in infancy by valiant performers in my native parts, and Anon was not long in London before he found his way to Lord's. The most charming sight he saw there was at an Eton and Harrow match. Among the dense crowd moving slowly round the ground stood a babe, an Etonian 'scug,' more properly attired than any other mortal may hope to be, but a-weary and asleep. In this sleep he stood, buffeted this way and that, but tile, socks, rosette, cane hooked on arm and all continued to function correctly – the perfect little gentleman.

In those days you could sit on the sward and watch the play as at a country match, but now I am such a swell that I look on from the little hotel on the left as you go in. We have got to know each other there, and I call the attendant I buy the ticket from George. Anon went alone to Lord's at first and did not dare speak to any one, but by his second year he was accompanied by friends, such as Gilmour, already darkly referred to and to be more fully exposed presently, and Marriott Watson with whom Anon afterwards wrote a play. Sometimes the three of them went for long tramps in Surrey, oftenmost to lovely Shere, in which village, 'over the butcher's shop,' Meredith told me he had written one of his novels. On these occasions they talked so much cricket that it began to be felt among them that they were hidden adepts at the game, and an ambition came over them to unveil. This was strengthened by the elderly appearance of the Shere team, whom they decided to challenge after letting them grow one year older. Anon was appointed captain (by chicanery it is said by the survivors), and he thought there would be no difficulty in getting a stout XI. together, literary men being such authorities on the willow. On the eventful day, however, he found out in the railway compartment by which they advanced upon Shere that he had to coach more than one of his players in the finesse of the game: which was the side of the bat you hit with, for instance. In so far as was feasible they also practised in the train. Two of the team were African travellers of renown, Paul du Chaillu of gorilla fame and the much loved Joseph Thomson of Masailand. When a name for the team was being discussed, Anon, now grown despondent, asked these two what was the 'African' for 'Heaven help us,' and they gave him 'Allahakbar.' So they decided to call themselves the Allahakbars, afterwards changed with complimentary intention to the Allahakbarries.

The Allahakbarries played a few matches yearly for several summers, that first one being the most ignominious. On the glorious hill-top of Albury where they were overwhelmed that day by Shere, Anon rashly allowed practice bowling, and one of the first balls sent down (by Bernard Partridge) loosened two teeth in the head of the prospective wicket-keeper, who was thus debarred from taking any further part in the game. Anon won the toss, to the indignation of his side, until they learned that this did not necessitate their going in first, and indeed he took the field to teach the Allahakbarries the game, first telling them what to do when the umpire said 'Over.' Unfortunately Shere had a horribly competent left-hander who at once set about smiting the bowling, and as this entailed constant changes in the field besides those ordered by the umpires the less gifted of the Allahakbarries decided that their captain knew no more about the rules than themselves. There were many other painful incidents, among them the conduct of du Chaillu, who stole away every few minutes and had to be pursued and brought back in custody.

[79]

It is immaterial now how many runs Shere made, but the score was a goodly one, and Partridge could do nothing to the teeth of any of them. At last, however, they were out, and the once long-looked-for time arrived for the Allahakbarries to go in. There was no longer a thirsty desire on the part of any of the team to open the innings, but in its place a passionate determination that this honour should be the captain's. I forget whether he yielded to the general wish, but at all events he ordered Marriott Watson to be No. 2, because all the time they were in the train, when others trembled, Marriott had kept saying gamely, 'Intellect always tells in the end.' For a lovely moment we thought it was to tell here, for he hit his first ball so hard that the Allahakbarries were at the beginning of a volley of cheers when they saw him coming out, caught at point by the curate. The captain amassed two. One man who partnered him was somewhat pedantic and before taking centre (as they were all instructed to do) signed to Anon that he had a secret to confide. It proved to be 'Should I strike the ball to however small an extent I shall run with consider- able velocity.' He did not have to run. The top scorer (as he tells to this day) was Gilmour, who swears he made five. The total was eleven.

The next time the Allahakbarries played Shere they won because they arrived two men short. They scoured the country in a wagonette, seeking to complete their team, and took with them, despite his protests, an artist whom they found in a field painting cows. They were still more fortunate in finding a soldier sitting with two ladies outside a pub. He agreed to accompany them if they would take the ladies also, and all three were taken. This unknown was the Allahakbarrie who carried the team that day to victory, and the last they saw of him he was sitting outside another pub with another two ladies.

Soon it became clear to Anon that the more distinguished as authors his men were the worse they played. Conan Doyle was the chief exception to this depressing rule, but after all, others did occasionally have their day, as when A. E. W. Mason, fast bowler, 'ran through' the opposing side, though one never knew in advance whether he was more likely to send the bails flying or to hit square leg in the stomach. Augustine Birrell once hit so hard that he smashed

[80]

the bat of Anon, which had been kindly lent him, and instead of grieving he called out gloriously, 'Fetch me some more bats.' Maurice Hewlett could sometimes look well set just before he came out. E. V. Lucas had (unfortunately) a style. Will Meredith would have excelled in the long field but for his way of shouting 'Boundary' when a fast ball approached him. Owen Seaman knew (or so he said) how to cut. Henry Ford was, even more than Tate, an unlucky bowler. Jerome once made two fours. Charles Whibley threw in unerringly but in the wrong direction. You should have seen Charles Furse as wicket-keeper, but you would have had to be quick about it as Anon had so soon to try some one else. Gilmour could at least continue to prate about his five. The team had no tail, that is to say, they would have done just as well had they begun at the other end. Yet when strengthened in the weaker points of their armour, namely in batting and bowling, by outsiders surreptitiously introduced, they occasionally astounded the tented field, as when by mistake they challenged Esher, a club of renown, and beat them by hundreds; an Allahakbarrie (whose literary qualifications I cannot remember) notching a century. Anon never would play Esher again, though they begged him to do so almost on bended knee.

Rivalry ran at its noblest when the Allahakbarries had their bouts with Broadway in Worcestershire, the scene of contests and suppers of Homeric splendour, at which fair ladies looked sympathetic as their heroes told of their deeds of long ago, including Gilmour's five. It was on such an occasion that Anon presented them with their Blues while Broadway's rafters rang. A. F. de Navarro and Turley Smith, both well-beloved, were the nominal captains of Broadway, but behind them stood the far more threatening figure of Worcester-shire's loveliest resident, Madame de Navarro, the famous Mary Anderson. Turley cared little which side won, nor did we, but far otherwise was it with that implacable one, who never (such is the glory of woman) could follow the game, despite deep study, and always called it 'crickets.' She had however a powerful way of wandering round the field with the Allahakbarries' top scorer, who when he came back would tell Anon sheepishly that he had promised to play for her in the second innings.

Anon twice made little books about the 'Broadway Week,' the first consisting of four pages, but the second was swollen to thirty, just as Wisden grows and grows. They were privately printed in tiny editions, and are rareties now, for most of them have gone for ever with the sound of the Allahakbarrie bat and ball. The first proudly acclaimed its vice-presidents,

> BEAU AUSTIN, ESQ.
> TERENCE MULVANEY, ESQ.
> OLD MEL, ESQ.
> SERGEANT TROY, ESQ.

Of the creators of these officials only one was himself a cricketer, Mr Meredith, and by his request Anon used to send him telegraphic communications about the state of the game, as he said he could not wait till morning. The second booklet was adorned with sketches, 'Broadway on a Match Day,' by Lindsay M'Arthur, in which not a dog or chicken shows, all live things being at the match; 'The Two Captains,' by Herman Herkomer, in which Madame de Navarro has just bowled Anon neck and crop; 'An Indispensable Part of their Luggage,' by E. T. Reid (a crate of ducks); Henry Ford's idea of 'How Partridge Sleeps Now' (in pads); and 'A Dream of Alfred Parsons by Himself' (in which he gets his hundred). There are also photographs, one of Birrell and Gilmour being compelled to go in first (at the end of a rope), and another, still more sinister, of Anon preparing a spot to suit his bowling. In the letterpress no member of the team escapes Anon's censure, and the whole ('Dedicated to our dear enemy, Mary de Navarro') ends with Owen Seaman's 'Ode to Himself on Making the Winning Hit':

> Bloody the battle, and the sun was hot,
> When on our ranks there fell an awful rot,
> One bearded warrior, playing like a Blue,
> Had made a prehistoric swipe for two,
> When three, his fellows, noted for their pluck,
> Through inadvertence got a paltry duck.
> Upon the war-path, which was far from flat,
> The foemen's champion had secured a hat,

[82]

And one might hear the dropping of a pin
When you, heroic sailor-soul, walked in.
Virgin, and chosen for your facial oddity,
In you your captain found a rare commodity,
Omitting not what other men omitted,
You went to make the winning hit and hit it.

Despite the picture of her capturing the Allahakbarrie captain's wicket, let it be put on record that Madame de Navarro herself never wielded the willow. She, however, watched avidly every ball sent down, and it is remembered how, in a certain single-innings match, when Anon said to her that she need watch no more as his side had already passed the Broadway score, she replied hopefully, 'Yes, but you have still several men to go in.' In the photograph of our Rosalind she is not inditing couplets to Orlando, but obviously drawing up a score for Anon's discomfiture. In their love for her the Allahakbarries tried to let her side win, but we were so accomplished it could not be done. I take back all my aspersions on the team. I remember now that we always won. The Allahakbarries were invincible.

The choice of such a name was apt. There is a certain fatalism in the Arabic affirmation, *Allahu akbar* (God is great), and as the u is the least important of the vowels it was easily left out.

Barrie's pen slipped slightly when he comments that 'Anon twice made little books about the "Broadway Week", the first consisting of four pages . . .'. That first precious rarity, produced in 1893, contains twice that number – Barrie was, no doubt, thinking of his original manuscript which comprised four pages – and it has nothing to do with Broadway. It does, though, have a lot to do with humour at the crease and the following winter copies were presented to a high-spirited company at the team's informal banquet, at Solferino's Restaurant in Soho (see pp. 84–93).

The cricket matches at Broadway started in 1897 in the following way. Mary Anderson, who had become disenchanted with her life as a Shakespearian actress, was delighted at the chance of renouncing the stage at the age of thirty and becoming instead a society hostess in the heart of the English countryside. Her marriage to Antonio 'Tony' de Navarro, a Papal Chamberlain and a member of the Basque aristocracy, gave her the necessary financial security and independence which enabled her to do that,

[83]

Allahakbarries

C.C.

1893

Patronesses .	. GRAHAM R. TOMSON.
	ELIZABETH ROBINS
	PENNELL
Captain's Girl .	. MADGE HENLEY
Hon. Presidents .	BEAU AUSTIN, Esq.
	TERENCE MULVANEY, Esq.
	OLD MEL, Esq.
	SERGEANT TROY, Esq.
Captain . .	. BARRIE, J. M.
Secretary & Treasurer	WATSON, H. B. MARRIOTT
Photographer .	. FREDERIC, HAROLD
Subsidised Crowd	. JEROME, J. K.
Skulker . .	. ANSTEY, F.
Umpire . .	. KENNAN, GEORGE
Committee .	. MESSRS. FORD, DOYLE,
	PARTRIDGE, TOMSON,
	WINTER, IVES, STUART
Professional .	. WHIBLEY
Ordinary Members .	FURSE, C. W.
Practice Grounds	. 20 ST. JOHN'S WOOD
	ROAD, AND *National*
	Observer OFFICE
Victories . .	. SHERE

THE ELEVEN

BARRIE (Capt.)

An incomparable Captain. The life and soul of his side. A treat to see him tossing the penny. Hits well off his pads. Once took a wicket.

WATSON

An invaluable man in the train going down. Very safe bat in the train. Loses confidence when told to go in.

TOMSON

Brilliant wicket - keeper. Often says "How's that?" Retires hurt amid loud cheers.

DOYLE

A grand bowler. Knows a batsman's weakness by the colour of the mud on his shoes.

WHIBLEY (Pro.)

Hits blooming hard, blooming high, and blooming seldom.

FORD

Nicknamed "Lost-ball Ford" because he and the ball are seldom in the same field.

WINTER

A safe run-getter when well set. Is never well set.

IVES

If he ever gets a ground to suit him, should take wickets.

PARTRIDGE

The Demon. Terrific delivery. Bowls all over the field. No one is safe. Breaks everything except the ball. Aims at the wicket and catches square leg in the stomach.

STUART

A colt. The surprise packet of the team.

FURSE

A dangerous man to have on your own side. Smokes in the field. Afraid of his captain.

FREDERIC

The worst batsman in the world. Equally at home with the ball.

HINTS

To the Team by their Captain

1

Don't practise on opponents' ground before match begins. This can only give them confidence.

2

Furse, hands out of pockets.

3

Each man when he goes in, to tap the ground with his bat.

4

Should you hit the ball, run at once. Don't stop to cheer.

5

No batsman is allowed to choose his own bowler. You needn't think it.

6

Partridge, when bowling, keep your eye on square leg.

7

Square leg, when Partridge is bowling, keep your eye on him.

8

If bowled first ball, pretend that you only came out for the fun of the thing,

and then go away and sit by yourself behind
the hedge.

9

Never forget that we beat Shere

REMARKS

On the Great Match at Shere

Our captain losing the toss in his usual crafty manner, immediately sent Shere in to bat. He set his field with exemplary coolness, and standing at cover point quickly dismissed Shere for the paltry total of 56. The wickets were nominally taken by Doyle, but entirely at the instigation of the captain.

The Allahakbarries opened their innings brilliantly. The captain going in first, in the person of Ford, showed complete mastery of the bowling, and rattled up

30 in a few minutes. He subsequently, in the persons of Doyle and Furse, played two brilliant innings, getting into double figures repeatedly. He received valuable help from Watson (who played a masterly innings of 2), from Whibley (who defied the best bowling in Shere for nearly a minute), from the hard-hitting Partridge (who would be invaluable against his own bowling), and from Tomson, who looked like scoring at any moment. It was a scene for Frederic to photograph, but he forgot to pull the string or let down the lid or something, and we all came out as a sunset in ye olden time.

and she soon gathered 'a very merry little colony' in Broadway – ambassa-
dors, artists, writers, musicians, any and everybody who was fun or famous
(preferably both) from Henry James, Paderewski and Sir Edward Elgar to
Maud Valerie White – for what seemed to be a non-stop house party. The
lady of the manor on a visit to London and 'seeing Sir James Barrie (then
J. M. Barrie), we "fixed up" a cricket match between his team, the
Allahakbarries, and a team of artists and singers which he wished me
to collect and captain'. Having become a gracious victim of Barrie's
enthusiasm for cricket, she goes on in her book, *A Few More Memories*:

The time for the great Test match arrived. One lovely morning Barrie (Captain), Owen Seaman, Augustine Birrell, Bernard
Partridge, A. E. W. Mason, S. Pawling, W. Meredith (son of
George Meredith), Gilmour, H. T. Ford (member of the well-
known cricketing family), E. T. Reid, A. N. Other, three reserves
and a bevy of their charming ladies, drove up to the village green,
waving and cheering in the true holiday humour. We were in the road
to welcome them, all like children out of school. My team included
H. Plunket Greene, Kennerley Rumford, Hermann Herkomer,
Frank Millet, Alfred Parsons, Tony, C. Turley Smith, C. Standring,
etc. no reserves. With the exception of three or four, there were no
real players.

Mary de Navarro remembers the match as being full of 'high nervous
tension, even consternation' and 'not at all merry':

It may seem suspicious, but I do not remember who won that year. I
know one of my men, Herkomer, was carried off the field in triumph.
So it looks as if *we* won. (I can only hope Barrie will not see this book.)
    The next summer there was another match, Conan Doyle being on
Barrie's side. It had come to my ears he had made 100 at Lord's. I,
therefore, wrote to Barrie before the match saying I hoped he would
not bring crack players, and that he should be like unto me in having
only 'amateurs' on his side, or words to that effect. I admit a
'centurion' made me nervous. I give his reply; it is a curious mixture
of 'vitriol and the milk of human kindness'.

[94]

'Dear Lady,

I am naturally greatly elated by your letter, and the kind things you insinuate rather than express. What particularly delights me is the note of uneasiness which you are at such pains to hide, but which bobs up repeatedly thro'out your bold defiance. The other day I showed my big dog to a child, and he kept saying, to give himself confidence, "He won't bite me; he won't bite me; I'm not afraid of his biting me," and it is obvious to the Allahakbarries that even in this manner do you approach me. They see also a wistfulness on your face as if, after having lorded it over mankind, you had at last met your match. Not, they say, that it will be your match. They read between the lines that in your heart you know it cannot be your match. Hence the wistfulness of your face as the summer draws near.

As one captain speaking to another, I would beg you not to let your team see that you are hopeless of their winning. It will only demoralize them *still further*. As for my score last year,[1] it was naturally a bitter pill to you, coming as it did somewhat unexpectedly, but it is unwise to let your mind brood on what I may do at our next engagement. As you say I may make five, but try to hope that by some accident I may not be in such superb form again.

I have no intention of changing my team this year. If I can get them I shall bring down last year's *winners* without alteration. That is, unless you, *as on another occasion*, get some of your musicians and artists from Oxford.

Also I offered last year not to put on Doyle and Pawling to bowl unless you put in your cracks, and when the fatal day arrives I am willing to make a similar offer again. I have always wanted the poorer players to have a chance, but your side would never agree.

Lastly, you say "Be then like unto me". If you would kindly tell me how it can be done, I shall proceed to do it right away.

Don't think by this that I mean I want to lure your players on to my side. I mean I want to be like you in your nobler moments. Teach me your fascinating ways. Teach me to grow your face. Teach me how you manage to be born anew every morning.

[1] It will be remembered that his score was a duck.

[95]

In short, I make you a sporting offer. Teach me all these things, and I will teach your team how to play cricket.
Awaiting your reply,
Yours ever,
J. M. Barrie.'

I believe (again I hope this book will escape him) Barrie was jealous of Tony's cricket. To have one of his best men 'Spread-eagled' by a beginner – whose games were baseball, racquets, tennis – must have been a shattering blow to him. I may be wrong in this belief, but of one thing I am certain: the brilliant Barrie was not a shining light in the cricket field. I never saw him make a single run. His speciality seemed to be in *poultry*.

Often in passing by the old ingle-nook in the hall, I can still see the slight figure of Barrie sitting in it, smoking a long church-warden pipe, his limpid eyes looking as innocent as those of a baby, while, as I learned to my sorrow, he was planning murder to my team: serenely puffing away, and death to the Broadway team in his heart!

It is thought that there were only twenty-two copies of the booklet printed, one for each member of the two teams, though a few more may have come off the press. In 1950, *Allahakbarries Book of Broadway Cricket 1899* attracted a reprint with a foreword by Don Bradman. Seven of the 'Hints' from *Allahakbarries C. C. 1893* replaced the section on 'Prizes' in the original (open to the female supporters and won by Daisy Partridge) and there was the addition of an introduction by Philip Comyns Carr. Carr's introduction is a shortened version of a twenty-minute talk that he gave on 'Barrie's Eleven' for the BBC Third Programme in June 1949. His script is here reproduced in full.

BARRIE'S ELEVEN

If you had met Barrie, a cricketer was about the last thing that you would have imagined him to be. For he was small, frail and sensitive, rather awkward in his movements, and there was nothing athletic in his appearance. And yet cricket was his great enthusiasm – not only watching cricket, but taking part in it. The French have an

[96]

expression, '*le violon d'Ingres*', for a hobby of this kind in great men, because Ingres, the painter, liked compliments on his violin playing, which was execrable, more than on his pictures. Well, cricket playing was certainly Barrie's '*violon d'Ingres*'. He would have given much to be good at it; but he was far less than good. So what did he do? Give up playing cricket? Never! He just turned his cricket into a joke.

That was very characteristic of Barrie. In himself, though not in his work, he sometimes seemed to be consciously absurd, for fear of being unconsciously ridiculous. He was timid and cautious. He could be a delightful talker, when he let himself go and felt sure he was among friends, but he could suddenly relapse into devastating silences, and I have seen him at his own table not utter a word during the whole meal. Even when the mood was on him to talk, he did so in a small and rather plaintive voice with a strong Scottish accent and a Highland lilt, so that when he spoke about a headache it sounded like a haddock; and one always had the impression that he was ready to retire suddenly, like a tiny lizard, into his cranny in the wall.

But it was in another way that Barrie's cricket was so typical of his humour and his personality. He was always acting a part, always representing himself as being something at once more cunning and also more simple than he really was. I do not know whether Barrie ever had the opportunity to learn cricket in his boyhood, either at the village school of Kirriemuir or at the Dumfries Academy; but I like to think that he had not, and that his enthusiasm for the game only started when he came to England and began to study the part of a member of the English middle class. It is true that it was typically a schoolboy's enthusiasm; and in this it was also in line with another part that he was always acting, that of his own Peter Pan, the boy who would not grow up. I should be exaggerating if I said that he wore a striped elastic belt with a snake clasp to hold up his flannels; but I am almost inclined to believe it, so much did his cricket suggest the schoolboy. He certainly wore around his boater straw hat the colours which he had chosen for the cricket club of which he was founder and captain. Such was Barrie the cricketer – or, if I may coin a word which I think describes him, Barrie the cricketeer.

I was myself a very junior member of the team, all the others being

The Allahakbarrie
Book of Broadway Cricket
for 1899.

TO OUR DEAR ENEMY,

MARY DE NAVARRO.

BROADWAY AS A CRICKET CENTRE.

In the leafy month of June, when old Sol progresses to his height of passion and sluggish draughts move gently through the vibrating light of a drowsy noontide, ruffling the dainty plumage of sweetly trilling songsters performing their ablutions in shaded pools, it is then that the panting climber of the precipitous paths of Parnassus longingly looks with lingering gaze over the seething masses of the madding crowd toiling intently in dusty thoroughfares to green fields dotted with white figures on reasonable terms.

Such a place is Broadway. The ozone of this village, which is charmingly situated between Court Farm and Russell House, dates back to the time of the Romans, who, with the help of Balbus, built a wall here. The name Broadway is of Roman origin, and is believed by the cognoscenti to be compounded of two words, *broad* and *way*. However this may be, it was certainly to Broadway that Caius retired when

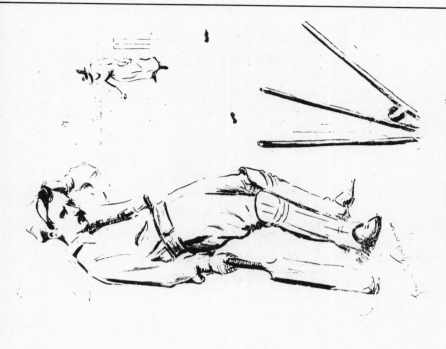

RESULT OF THE TEST MATCH, 1897.

he fled from the city. Here Cæsar probably played many fine innings of a Saturday afternoon. But all this was long ago, in the days of top hats and under-hand bowling. Coming to more recent times, and entering the village by the Evesham Road, the first object of interest at which we pause is Mr. Frank Millet. He is standing a little to the off. Immediately after leaving Mr. Millet, which we do with reluctance, but time is short and there is much to see, we scatter over his garden, strolling through the beautifully kept flower beds until we come to the Millet

QUACKUARY,

which is one of the sights of Broadway. The Quackuary is a sort of rustic steam-press in which the eggs laid by the Allahakbarries and their rivals are hatched by machinery. On the morning of a match all the female members of Russell House are up betimes hieing them to the cricket ground with aprons, into which they may be seen gathering the eggs. Many of the ducks which come waddling toward us are Allahakbarries, and they are quacking excitedly at the prospect of more little brothers and sisters.

6

We now return to our conveyance, and the courteous Jehu whipping up his horses we soon reach the

VILLAGE GREEN.

Pause here for a moment to observe the quaint house on the left, whose walls are well-nigh hidden by a magnificent specimen of the wisteria. H. J. Ford, O. Seaman, and A. E. W. Mason have stayed in that house. Almost directly opposite it is a more modern edifice, the erstwhile abode of A. Conan Doyle and S. Pawling. A straight line drawn between these two houses would represent the shortest way from the one to the other. Better, however, than stopping to draw this line, accompany us up the long street which now opens before us to the village hostelry, an ancient structure, heavy with historic associations. To the leg-side of the entrance is the

BANQUETING HALL OF THE ALLAHAKBARRIES,

and on the off is a narrow passage in which the first memorable meeting of the two captains took place. The stair leads to the chambers above. In one of these a Stuart king slept immediately before being caught and bowled for nothing. Edward T. Reed has also slept in this room.

Continuing our journey up the village street we pause for a moment at the shop where Gilmour bought a hat for a shilling. Well worth a visit also is the Curiosity Emporium across the way, where, if

ALLAHAKBARRIES EXAMINING THE STATE OF THE WICKET.

we are lucky, we may pick up some interesting relics, such as the spectacles left behind last year. We have now reached Court Farm, the

HEAD QUARTERS OF THE BROADWAY GANG,

B

and are shown over it by the mistress of the house, who, however, is looking a little pale to-day. That is Antonio de Navarro leaning against the wall for support. He looks pale. Messrs. Herkomer, Greene, Rumford, and Alfred Parsons form an interesting group in the Badminton Court. They are none of them feeling very well to-day. As we bid good-bye to our charming hostess, reminding her that we shall meet anon on the field, we notice that her hand trembles.

And now for the third Test Match.

BOWLERS AT PRACTICE.

WILL THEY DO THE HAT TRICK?

THE TEAM

For the 1899 Test Match.

When the spring of 1899 broke into summer it found the Allahakbarries already at the nets. Broadway had won the first Test Match (1897) by 1 run, Herkomer being responsible for the winning hit, and in the following year the Allahakbarries made hay of their opponents to the tune of 6 wickets, winning hit by O. Seaman, Esq. Feeling this year, therefore, ran very high, and in the exceptional circumstances the Allahakbarrie captain thought himself justified in arranging some trial matches for the first time in the history of the club. The first of these matches, which was played against the Artists (captained by E. A. Abbey), came off at Denmark Hill on a sullen wicket, and was remarkable for some tall scoring. Pawling made 34, Ford 32, and Pritchard 26. Others who played themselves into form in this match were

Partridge (4), Hornung (4), and Barrie (3). Reed (the popular Queen's Club pro.) and Mason were unfortunate with the bat, but they missed several catches in the field. Ford had the following highly creditable bowling analysis: 3 overs, 3 wides, 43 runs, and 0 wickets. On the other side Mr. Swinstead made a fair score.

Soon thereafter Mr. Barrie called a committee meeting to consider the composition of the team for the 1899 Test Match, present, himself and Reed. After a careful exchange of views the following were elected as a nucleus of the eleven: J. M. Barrie, Esq., Reed (E. T.). At the next meeting H. J. Ford and S. Pawling, with Partridge, were chosen; A. Conan Doyle was also mentioned at this meeting, but it was stated on authority that he had decided to devote himself henceforth to second-class cricket. These five are all Homeric men with the bat, and Ford, as he has shown this year, can trundle a bit, but so far the weak spot in the eleven (if any) is the bowling. It seemed wise to select some one for his bowling only, and after considering the claims of Pritchard, the choice fell on A. E. W. Mason. Now for a wicket-keeper. Hornung and Meredith have both kept the sticks at Broadway, and each had his backers. Another

AN INDISPENSABLE PART OF THEIR LUGGAGE.

good man is G. MacGregor, the Middlesex amateur, but the general feeling was in favour of a pro., and Meredith was finally fixed upon. We have as yet no suspicion of a tail, and to remedy this, O. Seaman was elected. We now want a hard hitter. Shall it be Gilmour or A. E. Stoddart? It was decided to play Gilmour if the pitch was treacherous, and Mr. Stoddart if it was sticky. For the tenth place a good all-round player who is at home on all kinds of wickets was the desideratum. Augustine Birrell is the very man. These with A. N. Other complete the team, which is thus composed as follows :

J. M. Barrie, Esq. (Forfarshire) (*Capt.*).
H. J. Ford, Esq. (Middlesex).
S. Pawling, Esq. (Berkshire).
A. E. W. Mason, Esq. (Kent).
O. Seaman, Esq. (Surrey).
A. Birrell, Esq. (Lancashire).
A. N. Other, Esq. (Yorkshire).

WITH

Reed, E. T. (Kent).
Meredith, W. (Surrey).
Partridge, J. B. (Middlesex).
Gilmour, Thomas (Lincolnshire).

Reserves—Messrs. Pritchard, MacGregor, and Stoddart.

ALLAHAKBARRIES COMPELLING BIRRELL AND GILMOUR TO GO IN FIRST.

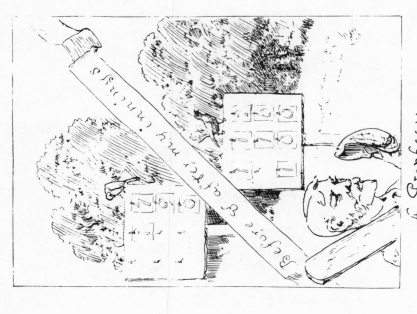

Before & after my innings

A Prophesy

BY ALFRED PARSONS.

THE NIGHT BEFORE THE MATCH.

AN ALLAHAKBARRIE PREPARING A SPOT TO SUIT HIS BOWLING.

FORECAST

Of the Allahakbarrie Score in the 1899 Test Match.

This annual engagement, which is now recognized as a first-class fixture, came off to-morrow at Broadway in ideal cricketing weather. By 11.15 the pavilion was thronged with beautiful women and brainy men.

16

A perfect wicket, a little on the creamy side, had been prepared by the groundsmen, Millet and Navarro.

Barrie (*Capt.*) again won the toss, and after examining the wicket elected to go in. He did not go in himself.

The Broadway team took the field at 11.30. They look a gamey lot.

I have just learned that Barrie (*Capt.*) expects the wicket to play queerly.

Amid loud cheers Seaman and Gilmour now strode to the wickets.

Barrie is being severely criticised for sending Gilmour in first.

Seaman is carrying his bat over his shoulder, which creates a favourable impression.

Gilmour is to take first over. He looks pale but determined.

In a strange silence Plunket Greene, who is trundling from the Bramall Lane end, sends down the first ball.

The next man in is Ford.

Ford stands seven feet in his stockings, and meets all balls in the middle of the pitch. Curiously enough, Ford was originally played as a bowler.

Ford has opened his account by pulling Greene beautifully all round the wickets for 3.

A complete change has now come over the game.

It is Seaman's turn to face the music. Seaman shapes very badly. I fear he will not be a stayer.

The last ball of the over was lifted by Seaman over his head for 2 (all run).

Seaman is now well set.

Ford has hit Smith all along the ground for 1.

The bowling is now tied in a knot.

Seaman is very uncomfortable with Smith's curly ones. He made some shocking strokes. I expect to see him go at any moment.

Seaman has cut Smith for 3, and driven him to the ropes for 4. I shall be surprised if Seaman does not give Broadway more trouble to-day.

The separation, however, came from the other end. In lifting a ball to deep mid-off Seaman was smartly caught by Parsons at square leg standing back. He had compiled a very stylish 9 in twelve and a half minutes, and received an ovation.

13 for 2. It is still anybody's game.

The ladye Harpe de Navarro throweth ye gloue to ye puissant Sir James of Kirriemuir, and challengeth hym to combat in ye tented field.

BP

RESULT OF THE TEST MATCH, 1898.

Meredith is Ford's next partner. He is a graceful bat.

13 for 3.

Pawling is the next to wield the willow.

The score now reads 13 for 4. It is Ford who is out.

Reed has joined Pawling, and from his third ball he gave a palpable chance to Herkomer at cover point, but it was not held. Profiting by this escape Reed fluked the ball finely through the slips for **2**, and manipulated it to the on for a dainty single. He was then out l.b.w. The let-off has cost Broadway dear.

The next man in was Barrie (*Capt.*). On returning he received an ovation.

Partridge and Pawling now came together. Partridge is wearing his new pads, but they impede his progress to the wickets, and I fear he will not be a stayer.

Pawling is playing with his scoring bat.

The long innings of Pawling has been at last brought to a close. He has scraped together 6. His wickets were spread-eagled by Navarro. Pawling retired much dissatisfied with the ruling of the umpire.

20

On Mason's joining Partridge the score stood thus: 22 for 7.

The stand of the innings now took place.

Partridge opened the ball by bagging a brace of lovely cuts, each for 3 and both off his pads.

Partridge has just despatched the sphere to the boundary. It was a glide off his pads. I am confident that Partridge's pads will stand him in good stead to-day.

Mason is content to keep up his end and leave the scoring to Partridge.

The score rises so rapidly that the figures dance on the telegraph board.

Smith is bowling with his head. He has just sent down a very hot one, but Partridge opened his pads to it and a 4 accrued.

The 50 is now up, and the scoring is terrific. Partridge has laid aside his bat and is kicking out.

With two 3's and a beauty to the ropes for 4 Partridge has sent up the 60. All bowling is alike to him to-day. The 70 is now up.

Partridge is twenty-one years of age. He played many good games for his school, and first attracted the attention of Barrie when practising at the nets.

He made his first appearance for the Allahakbarries in 1893, and got his blue in the same year. He stands 5 feet 10½ inches in his pads.

The 80 is now up. In a single over from Parsons Partridge snicked him to mid-off, smashed him to leg, hurled him among the crowd, and twice lifted him in the air and banged him hard against the pavilion. This sent up the 100 amid loud applause.

There was an interval of a few minutes at this point to enable Partridge to be photographed.

I have had a brief conversation with Partridge. He tells me that he never played his own game until to-day. He resides in the N.W. district, and is qualified for Middlesex, but cannot afford the time for three-day matches. His telegraphic address is "PADS, LONDON."

On the game being resumed Mason appeared without his bat, and Partridge, who is much annoyed, appealed to the umpire. The decision was given against him, however, and Mason is trying to play Partridge's game.

Partridge continues to give them beans. Off two overs he has scored three 4's and four 3's. The 130 is now up.

In winter Partridge is by profession an artist. He

is on the ground staff of "Punch." He is a modest unaffected fellow, and very popular among his brother pros. According to "Who's Who" he has as yet published nothing, but contemplates a work to be entitled "A New Way to Play Old Cricket." He is fond of all outdoor sports. He also bikes, but whether in pads I cannot say. He is a non-smoker. His position at the wickets is easy and alert, and he has a large variety of strokes, but he is perhaps best with the right leg. He plays with a very straight pad.

Mason is out, caught and bowled, and has lent invaluable assistance, which must not be judged by the amount of his runs. His full score stands thus : I.

The remaining batsmen are Birrell and 'Tother. The end is now close at hand.

Herkomer is deputed to bowl, and is mixing them all he knows. The first ball Birrell got went through him. The second, third, and fourth hit him on the chest. Herkomer has found the spot.

Birrell is out.

Tother now whipped in. He evidently means to lay on the wood.

Tother missed his first ball and ran, but he

THE DROOPING FIGURE IS EDWARD T. REED.

D

was given out. His has been a short but merry innings.

The tenth wicket fell with the total at 132.

Partridge carried out his pads for a superb 110.

FRANK MILLET, ESQ., SNEERING AT THE PLAY OF ALFRED PARSONS, ESQ.

Lest the Forecast should be wrong in some of its details this page has been left blank, so that the fortunate possessor of this work may append the scores actually made.

O. SEAMAN AND THE BAT HE DID IT WITH.

THE WINNING HIT.

An Ode to Myself on making 2 not out in the Test Match of 1898.

By Owen Seaman.

Bloody the battle, and the sun was hot,
When on our ranks there fell an awful rot.
One bearded warrior, playing like a Blue,
Had made a prehistoric swipe for two,

29

PARTRIDGE'S GOLDEN DREAM.

When three, his fellows, noted for their pluck,
Through inadvertence got a paltry duck.
Upon the warpath, which was far from flat,
The foeman's champion had secured a hat,
And one might hear the dropping of a pin
When you, heroic sailor-soul, walked in.
Virgin, and chosen for your facial oddity,
In you your captain found a rare commodity,
Omitting not what other men omitted,
You went to make the winning hit and hit it.

EDWARD T. REED SAYS HE COULD PLAY THAT
BOWLING ALL DAY.

PRIZES.

The Committee have the honour to announce
that valuable prizes will be presented to those lady
members of the Allahakbarrie Troupe who solve the
following problems. The answers must be filled up
in the train going down :

1. How many runs will the Allahakbarries score?

MASON AND MEREDITH WONDERING WHETHER
THEY SHOULD PLAY A FORCING GAME.

31

2. Of these how many will be contributed by Gilmour, Seaman, Meredith, and Barrie respectively?

3. Which of the Allahakbarries will take the first wicket?

4. Which of them will make the first boundary?

5. Who will make top score?

6. Who will bring off the first catch?

7. Will Birrell be caught or bowled or fall over his wicket?

8. How many ducks will there be?

9. How many will get into double figures besides Reed?

10. Which bowler will take most wickets?

11. Ford is to be put on for three overs. Will he beat his Denmark Hill record, and if so, by how many?

NOTE.—These questions refer to the first innings only of the Allahakbarries. The competitor must sign her name at the foot of this page, which must be countersigned by the captain.

THE PRIDE OF BROADWAY.

older and distinguished men – I do not say all distinguished cricketers, though a few almost were, and this was part of Barrie's joke. I
came to join the club in this way. It had not been long in existence in
1897, and what I think must have been one of its earliest matches was
a game played in that year in the now famous village of Broadway, in
Worcestershire, between a resident team of painters, brought
together by the beautiful Madame de Navarro, who was the American actress Mary Anderson, and a visiting team of literary men, led
by Barrie. That game Barrie lost; but when there was a question of a
return match the following year, he was determined not to lose again.
This he rather looked like doing, as he could no longer count upon
what had been his chief tower of strength, the colossus, Conan
Doyle. 'Doyle has gone into second class cricket,' he explained. And
it was literally true. So he wrote to me – I was then in my last year at
Oxford – and asked me whether I could bring along two men, whose
literary qualifications would pass muster, but who could anyway play
cricket. Incidentally, he invited me to join the club.

As I knew Broadway and its artist colony very well, I was
delighted. I turned up with my two cricketers, and we won the
match, though neither side, if I remember right, scored more than
thirty-five for two innings, and the winning hit was made by neither
of my Oxford friends, but by Owen Seaman, the editor of *Punch*. He
afterwards celebrated the event in verse.

After the match, Barrie gave a dinner at the Lygon Arms to the two
teams, with their wives and other lady members of the colony, and,
later in the evening, Frank Millet, the American painter, had a dance
in his studio at Russell House. Millet was really the founder of the
colony, which had originally included two much more famous
American artists. These were Abbey, who also once got up a cricket
match against Barrie, but not at Broadway, and Sargent. It was in the
garden of Frank Millet's Russell House that Sargent painted his first
really successful picture, 'Carnation, lily, lily, rose'. The models for
that brilliant impression of Japanese lanterns being lit at dusk were
the two young daughters of a very English artist, finest of Dickens
illustrators, Fred Barnard. His widow had joined the colony, as had
the also very English landscape and garden painter, Alfred Parsons.

Before the match, Barrie had presented each of us with a copy of his rules of cricket. The only rule that I can remember is, 'When you hit the ball, run. Don't stop to cheer.' After the dinner, he made a speech, at the end of which he threw across the table to each of us what he called 'your blue', a silk cap of the most hideous assortment of colours that he had been able to purchase at the shop in Regent Street where all the club colours in the world were sold. As it happened, they were also the colours of a Brasenose College luncheon club, to which I and one of my two Oxford friends belonged. To every member of the team, Barrie recalled his achievement in the match. 'You,' he said to one, 'scored a good single in the first innings, but you were not so successful in the second.' 'You,' he said to the opposing team, 'ran up a fine total of fourteen, and you nearly won.'

He began his speech by telling us how he came to form the club. 'One day,' he said, 'I was walking along a country lane with Gilmour, and he saw a bird in a hedge. And he threw a stone, and it hit the hedge. And from that we went on to talk of country sports. Perhaps,' he continued, 'you would like to know how the club was given its name, the Allahakbarries. I had taken a saloon carriage to travel by train to our first match, and on the way I was giving the boys a few preliminary instructions – which end of the bat to hold, and so forth. Then someone said we ought to have a name, and he suggested this one. "Why?" I asked. "Well," he answered, "it is the Moorish for God help us." Of course,' said Barrie, 'I had to be guided by some principles in choosing the members of the club. The principles were these. With regard to the married men, it was because I liked their wives, and with regard to the single men, it was for the oddity of their personal appearance.'

The Broadway match was repeated the following year, 1899. For that occasion, Barrie had prepared and privately printed 'The Allahakbarrie book of Broadway cricket for 1899'. This little parchment-covered and illustrated booklet now has a fantastic collector's value. The copy which I still possess carries the signatures of all the members of the team. They begin with Barrie himself, who puts 'capt.' in brackets after his name. They go on with his friend Gilmour, then E. T. Reid and Bernard Partridge, the *Punch* artists, Owen Seaman, their editor, Henry Ford, the illustrator and member

[116]

of a famous cricketing family, Hesketh-Prichard, who had played for his county as well as being a man of letters, A. E. W. Mason, the novelist, Will Meredith, son of George Meredith, and himself a member of the publishing firm of Constable, Sydney Pawling, of Heinemann's, another publishing house. Then comes my own signature and finally that of Augustine Birrell, who modestly adds 'on approval' in brackets after his name. I rather fancy that he did not actually play, though he was certainly there; for it will be noted that there are twelve names, and not eleven. It will also be noted that there are artists as well as literary men in the team, so that the match is no longer between these two professions. It is just Broadway versus the Allahakbarries.

The illustrations to the booklet begin with a drawing of Broadway's main street, absolutely empty. It is given the title 'Broadway on a match day'. The next is by Herman Herkomer. It is called 'result of the Test Match 1897', and it shows Barrie scratching his head as he is clean bowled, apparently by Madame de Navarro in person and in a large feathered hat. Other drawings include one by E. T. Reid, called 'an indispensable part of their luggage'. It is of a porter at Evesham Station, roaring with laughter as he contemplates an open crate of quacking ducks, labelled 'Allahakbarrie Cricket Club'. There is one by Alfred Parsons, called 'A Prophesy', with his self portrait carrying out his bat for a hundred: and one, very heraldic, by Bernard Partridge, of 'The Ladye Marye de Navarro', in striped blazer and cap, challenging a small but defiant 'Sir James of Kirriemuir', wearing his pads and crowned with the laurels of victory after the Test Match of 1898. Pads again form the main subject of Ford's sketch, called 'Partridge's golden dream'. It represents Bernard Partridge, whose one run the previous year had been scored by a ball glancing off his pads. He is asleep with his pads on, and dreams of numberless pads, come to life, and hitting the ball with bats.

The most amusing of the illustrations are, however, the photographs – of course taken the previous year. They are amusing chiefly on account of the titles given to them. Mason and Meredith are shown 'wondering whether they should play a forcing game'. Antonio de Navarro and Plunket Greene, the singer, are presented as 'the pride of Broadway'. A picture of an obvious tug of war has the caption 'Allahakbarries compelling Birrell and Gilmour to go in first.' A photo of Barrie and Partridge, clearly throwing something, is called 'Bowlers at practice. Will they do the hat trick?' But best of all, I think, is a snapshot of Barrie himself in his straw hat, pressing down a large garden fork into the ground with his foot. It has the title, 'The night before the match. An Allahakbarrie preparing a spot to suit his bowling.'

Except for Seaman's verses in commemoration of his own winning hit the previous year, the text of the booklet, though anonymous, is obviously by Barrie. The first chapter is headed 'Broadway as a cricket centre', and it begins, 'In the leafy month of June, when old Sol progresses to his height of passion'. It then goes back to the historic days when Broadway was a Roman road, and, in its own words, 'Caesar probably played many a fine innings here of a Saturday afternoon; but that was long ago, in the days of top hats and underhand bowling'. After taking the reader up the village street, past what is called 'the banqueting hall of the Allahakbarries' – that is to say, the Lygon Arms Hotel – to Court Farm, the home of Mary de Navarro, and here described as the 'headquarters of the Broadway gang', the author discusses the formation of his team. He shows how Ford was selected once more as a bowler because in the last match he had the 'highly creditable analysis of three overs, three wides, forty-three runs and nought wickets'. He says that the Committee hesitated in their search for a hard hitter between Gilmour and A. E. Stoddart, who as a batsman was the Denis Compton of that day, but decided to play Gilmour as the pitch was treacherous; and he adds that Augustine Birrell was chosen for the tenth place as 'a good all round player, who is at home on all kinds of wickets'.

The author then gives a forecast description of what will be the Allahakbarrie first innings in the 1899 match. 'In a strange silence Plunket Greene, who is trundling from the Bramall Lane end, sends down the first ball. The next man in is Ford.' A little later, we learn that Seaman, lifting a ball to deep mid-off, is smartly caught by Parsons at square leg. 'He had compiled,' says the book, 'a very stylish nine in twelve and a half minutes, and received an ovation.

Thirteen for two. It is still anybody's game. Meredith is Ford's next partner. He is a graceful bat. Thirteen for three. It is now Pawling's turn to wield the willow. Thirteen for four. It is Ford who is out. The next man in was Barrie (Capt.) On returning he received an ovation. The long innings of Pawling has at last been brought to a close. In all he has scraped together a total of six. His wicket was spread-eagled by Navarro. Pawling retired much dissatisfied with the ruling of the umpire.'

The forecast proceeds, 'Now Mason is out, caught and bowled. He has lent invaluable assistance, which must not be judged by the amount of his runs. His full score stands thus: one. The next man is Birrell. Herkomer is deputed to bowl, and is mixing them all he knows. The first ball Birrell got went right through him. The second, third and fourth hit him on the chest. Herkomer has found the spot. Birrell is out. A.N. Other' – that was myself – 'now whipped in. He evidently means to lay on the wood. A. N. Other missed his first ball and ran, but he was given out. His has been a short but merry innings.'

Such was the forecast. The booklet leaves a blank page, so that – in the words of its author – 'the fortunate possessor of this work may append the scores actually made'. But the reality was very little different. I think Pawling went into double figures, and I fancy Prichard did too; but the rest scored, or failed to score, much as had been predicted. What the forecast did not give was the excitement and spirit of the match. I cannot say that the crowd was large; and the interest of the feminine part of it – which predominated – was perhaps directed more towards urging middle-aged husbands to put on sweaters or blazers and not catch chills than towards the play or the result. To be sure, some members of both teams were younger men, and were really cricketers. I fancy their chief anxiety must have been not to appear to be tempering the wind to those who were not, and yet to give them a chance. Of course, the hope upon which the hearts of all of us, on both sides, were centred was that Barrie himself would make some runs, for we all loved him. But alas, he never did.

I believe another match was arranged at Broadway for the following year, but I am not sure that it was ever played. For the thing had begun to be talked about, and there was a prospect of the presence of more strangers, and even newspaper men, than the family party would have liked.

I continued to see Barrie long after I had ceased to play cricket for him; and I remember that one night, at dinner at my father's house, he was deploring the enormous popular success of Marie Corelli. 'Of course you're right, Jimmie,' said my father, 'but after all, she is alive.' 'Yes,' drawled Barrie, 'that's where I blame her.'

I think it was the same night that he told my father that when he and his wife parted, he had said to her that she could keep their Peter Pan country cottage in the Surrey pinewoods and all the contents as they stood, except one little thing. This he said he could come and fetch at a time which he fixed, so that she could avoid meeting him. 'She must have wondered,' he said to my father, 'what I was taking away in my small black bag.' It was the letters which George Meredith had written to him.

Black Lake Cottage, near Farnham, had been bought by Mary Barrie in the spring of 1900 and with its extensive south lawn became the new 'home' ground for the Allahakbarries. The scorebook of the team, with the signature 'J. M. Barrie, 133, Gloucester Rd.' on the title page, is kept at Lord's and reveals that between 1899 and 1903 games were played against Artists, Shere Fire Brigade, Broadway, Mr Morris's XI, Conan Doyle's team, Mr Horne's XI, Esher, The Punch Bowl, the Pasture Wood Club and the Royal Engineers, Chatham, at such venues as Kensington Park, Shackleford, Dorking, Denmark Hill and Frensham Bowl. There was even a Duffers' Match between two highly competitive Allahakbarrie sides.

For some of the games, there were two prizes offered – one for ten shillings and one for five shillings – to anyone who could guess the total sum of the two innings, if completed. A sentence in pencil on the last page of the scorebook promises that 'anyone drawing wife of 1st or 2nd scorer gets half the stakes'.

The 'stylish' E. V. Lucas relates how the Allahakbarries were not too 'distressed by defeat. J. C. Snaith, who had been tried for Notts, was our trump card with the ball, but Barrie bowled slow left, with an action very like J. C. White of Somerset and England, and had to be watched. Will Meredith, George Meredith's son, kept wicket with a magnificent composure and disdain of byes; C. T. Smith (who under the name of Charles Turley writes some of the best school stories) fielded in the slips like a county player; Conan Doyle, who was very good, was our best all-rounder, and Harry Graham, the librettist, batted as though he had been properly taught. Another useful man was Walter Frith, son of the painter of "Derby Day". In addition to regular players, there were occasional extra men, such as Charles Whibley, who was said by his captain, adapting a well-known phrase, to hit "blooming hard, blooming high and blooming seldom", and Hewlett, who used to turn out in perfect flannels but was not proficient.

'Among the artists, who, since they never do anything to tire them, were always stronger than their adversaries, the chief scores were made by Henry Ford, the illustrator of Andrew Lang's fairy books. They also had, in G. H. Swinstead, a formidable performer with both bat and ball. H. H. La Thangue was one of their keenest supporters. E. A. Abbey was usually captain, bringing into the game all his American energy and a terrifying velocity in throwing which he had acquired at baseball; but otherwise he was not to be feared.'

Lucas's mention of Edwin Abbey, who painted the great series of mural decorations which adorn Boston Public Library in Massachusetts and which illustrate 'The Quest and Achievement of the Holy Grail' – ruined, incidentally, by being set in a room with an uncovered light – brings to mind an encounter at Lord's, Artists v. Authors, in which he and Barrie were on opposing sides. Albert Kinross, whose *The Unconventional Cricketer* was produced in 1930, remarks that each side liked the two men so much that they tried not to get them out. Neither of them appeared to take the game very seriously and Barrie 'sported a most businesslike cap and blazer done in colours of his own invention'.

In one of the games between the Artists and the Writers, Barrie arranged that the two worst batsmen in each XI should begin their side's innings by facing the two worst bowlers, and that the latter should not be taken off until a wicket fell. This clever move enabled the Writers to mount a substantial first-wicket stand – Barrie being one of the batsmen – even though the total comprised more wides than runs. At another match, one famous novelist turned out in frock coat and cricket cap, to the vast amusement of all and sundry. On that day too, a mischievous journalist reported that 'Mr Barrie played superbly for not out o'.

After Abbey's death, Barrie wrote that 'he would have tried to stop a thunderbolt to save the third run. The only fault he found in cricket was that it was not sufficiently dangerous. He tried to remedy this. As soon as you struck the ball you remembered Abbey and flung yourself on your face.'

The Allahakbarries carried on playing intermittently up until just before the First World War. Their last fixture was against E. V. Lucas's XI at

Downe House in 1913, and after stumps were drawn both sides journeyed by brake and steam train to London for a supper at the Savoy Grill. The players on that occasion included a few old faithfuls, Tom Gilmour and Will Meredith among them, and some relatively 'new blood', Denis Mackail, A. A. Milne and Charles Tennyson. Tennyson, talking on the Home Service nearly fifty years later, remembered an Allahakbarrie encounter against the Punchbowl Club at Frensham. Evidently, the club lived up to its name by filling a bathcan full of punch and placing it by the side of the pitch, so that whenever a fielder felt the need of liquid refreshment he could go and help himself. A lot did, liberally. At dinner that evening, Barrie commented: 'Did you notice that when one member of the Punchbowl team was hit on the shin, the whole team swelled?'

Before temporarily deserting the Allahakbarries, we should not forget that glorious piece of eccentric behaviour in which Arthur Conan Doyle nearly succeeded in revising the rules of cricket. A. A. Thomson in *Odd Men In* relates how the Allahakbarries had made 72 and had taken nine enemy wickets for exactly the same total.

At this point, Arthur started to bowl. There were indignant cries from the pavilion and the entire batting side emerged, arguing fiercely. Arthur, you must understand, was the only effective bowler on the side and at this critical juncture, in sheer excitement and with no evil intent, he was beginning a new over, having just taken his ninth wicket with his last ball at the other end. For years afterwards, Arthur claimed to be the first bowler who had attempted this felony (though by accident) and was a little hurt when a quarter of a century later Warwick Armstrong stole his thunder by breaking the same law in a Test match. In point of historic fact, Arthur was not allowed to bowl his second over, anyway. With all eleven opponents swarming round him, waving their copies of the Laws of Cricket, Arthur bowed to the storm and dropped his ball. To prevent a riot, another bowler was put on and the enemy won forthwith by a wide and four overthrows.

The unparalleled power that a game of bat and ball can have over the minds of men never ceases to amaze those for whom the allurement of cricket is indiscernible. Many were astonished to find the only thing that could be relied upon without fail to rekindle Barrie after one of his customary long melancholic bouts of silence was to talk cricket. His devoted secretary for so many years, Lady Cynthia Asquith, whose unrealized ambition was to lead a women's cricket team against the Australians, tells in her *Portrait of Barrie* of how in particular he loved reliving the old days with the Allahakbarries (at his flat in Adelphi Terrace in which there was room enough to play cricket) in the company of the excitable, extravagant but always endearing fellow-writer and team mate, Charles Whibley:

'No one,' said Barrie, 'no one threw in harder than you, Charles, unerringly in the wrong direction, but then Conan Doyle was the only exception to the depressing rule that the more successful were the members of my team as authors, the worse they played.'

'Anyway, I never let the blasted ball hit me!' boasted Whibley.

They exchanged reminiscences of that engaging fancy cricketer, Augustine Birrell, who, Barrie said, had required a little coaching in the finesse of the game – for instance, which was the side of the bat you hit with, and what to do when the umpire shouted 'Over'.

'D'you remember, Charles?' said Barrie, taking an extra long pull at his pipe and lolling back in his chair with one leg tucked under the other, as is his queer contortionary way when he feels most at ease, and is about to drop into his 'I always remember' vein.

'D'you remember when, at the very beginning of his innings, Birrell broke the bat kindly lent him by his captain, and, exultant at its having been struck by the ball, and quite ungrieving about my ruined bat, waved it towards the pavilion and shouted "Bring me some more bats!"'

CRICKET WITH THE BOYS

'THE horror of my boyhood was that I knew a time would come when I must give up games, and how it was to be done, I knew not . . .' That cry from the heart says so much and yet so little about its author. The plurality of Barrie's personality, cogently described by Cynthia Asquith, is often too conveniently defined in unqualified terms. In a letter to her husband, soon after starting to work for Barrie, she wrote: 'As for the legend of his being himself "The Boy who wouldn't grow up", I see no evidence whatsoever of this. On the contrary, he strikes me as more than old. In fact, I doubt whether he ever *was* a boy. But then, for the matter of that, Peter Pan isn't a boy, is he? He's a wish-fulfilment projection in fable form of the kind of mother – Barrie's an expert at her – who doesn't want her son to grow up.'

Barrie's love of children, the inescapable sadness at not having any of his own, partly the result of tendentious kirk-like strictures at his mother's knee, was manifested in strange ways. His 'adoption' of the five Llewelyn Davies boys, who were the sons of the actor Gerald du Maurier's sister, went to extreme lengths. The Davies family, or more exactly, the elder boys, were the catalyst for *The Little White Bird*, in which Peter Pan made his first appearance.

Barrie used to take his big St Bernard, Luath, for regular walks in Kensington Gardens and there met the children in the company of their nanny. Before long, they were taking part in all sorts of games, spyo, smuggle bools, kick-bonnety, peeries capey-dykey and, of course, cricket; however, there was a long gestation period before their pastimes reached a wider public. Cricket was called Crickets in the Gardens though not on the printed page:

Between the well and the Round Pond are the cricket-pitches, and frequently the choosing of sides exhausts so much time that there is scarcely any cricket. Everybody wants to bat first, and as soon as he is out he bowls unless you are the better wrestler, and while you are wrestling with him the fielders have scattered to play at something else. The Gardens are noted for two kinds of cricket: boy cricket, which is real cricket with a bat, and girl cricket, which is with a racquet and the governess. Girls can't really play cricket, and when you are watching their futile efforts you make funny sounds at them. Nevertheless, there was a very disagreeable incident one day when some forward girls challenged David's team, and a disturbing creature called Angela Clare sent down so many yorkers that – However, instead of telling you the result of that regrettable match I shall pass on hurriedly to the Round Pond, which is the wheel that keeps all the Gardens going.

On another day, there was another game. David (George Davies) was a doughty opponent.

THE CRICKET MATCH

I think there has not been so much on a cricket match since the day when Sir Horace Mann walked about Broad Ha'penny agitatedly cutting down the daisies with his stick. And, be it remembered, the heroes of Hambledon played for money and renown only, while David was champion of a lady. A lady! May we not prettily say of two ladies? There were no spectators of our contest except now and again some loiterer in the Gardens who little thought what was the stake for which we played, but cannot we conceive Barbara standing at the ropes and agitatedly cutting down the daisies every time David missed the ball? I tell you, this was the historic match of the Gardens.

David wanted to play on a pitch near the Round Pond with which he is familiar, but this would have placed me at a disadvantage, so I insisted on unaccustomed ground, and we finally pitched stumps in the Figs. We could not exactly pitch stumps, for they are forbidden in the Gardens, but there are trees here and there which have chalkmarks on them throughout the summer, and when you take up your position with a bat near one of these you have really pitched stumps. The tree we selected is a ragged yew which consists of a broken trunk and one branch, and I viewed the ground with secret satisfaction, for it falls slightly at about four yards' distance from the tree, and this exactly suits my style of bowling.

I won the toss and after examining the wicket decided to take first knock. As a rule when we play the wit at first flows free, but on this occasion I strode to the crease in an almost eerie silence. David had taken off his blouse and rolled up his shirt-sleeves, and his teeth were set, so I knew he would begin by sending me down some fast ones.

His delivery is underarm and not inelegant, but he sometimes tries a round-arm ball, which I have seen double up the fielder at square leg. He has not a good length, but he varies his action bewilderingly, and has one especially teasing ball which falls from the branches just as you have stepped out of your ground to look for it. It was not, however, with his teaser that he bowled me that day. I had notched a three and two singles, when he sent me down a medium to fast which got me in two minds and I played back to it too late. Now, I am seldom out on a really grassy wicket for such a meagre score, and as David and I changed places without a word, there was a cheery look on his face that I found very galling. He ran in to my second ball and cut it neatly to the on for a single, and off my fifth and sixth he had two pretty drives for three, both behind the wicket. This, however, as I hoped, proved the undoing of him, for he now hit out confidently at everything, and with his score at nine I beat him with my shooter.

The look was now on my face.

I opened my second innings by treating him with uncommon respect, for I knew that his little arm soon tired if he was unsuccessful, and then when he sent me loose ones I banged him to the railings. What cared I though David's lips were twitching?

When he ultimately got past my defence, with a jumpy one which broke awkwardly from the off, I had fetched twenty-three, so that he needed twenty to win, a longer hand than he had ever yet made. As I gave him the bat he looked brave, but something wet fell on my hand, and then a sudden fear seized me lest David should not win.

At the very outset, however, he seemed to master the bowling, and

[126]

soon fetched about ten runs in a classic manner. Then I tossed him a Yorker which he missed and it went off at a tangent as soon as it had reached the tree. 'Not out,' I cried hastily, for the face he turned to me was terrible.

Soon thereafter another incident happened, which I shall always recall with pleasure. He had caught the ball too high on the bat, and I just missed the catch. 'Dash it all!' said I irritably, and was about to resume bowling, when I noticed that he was unhappy. He hesitated, took up his position at the wicket, and then came to me manfully. 'I am a cad,' he said in distress, 'for when the ball was in the air I prayed.' He had prayed that I should miss the catch, and as I think I have already told you, it is considered unfair in the Gardens to pray for victory.

My splendid David! He has the faults of other little boys, but he has a noble sense of fairness. 'We shall call it a no-ball, David,' I said gravely.

I suppose the suspense of the reader is now painful, and therefore I shall say at once that David won the match with two lovely fours, the one over my head and the other to leg all along the ground. When I came back from fielding this last ball I found him embracing his bat, and to my sour congratulations he could at first reply only with hysterical sounds. But soon he was pelting home to his mother with the glorious news.

And that is how we let Barbara in.

In a broadcast in the General Overseas Service in 1952, Pamela Maude, daughter of old-time thespian Cyril Maude, told of how Mr Barrie 'looked sad' when he made jokes. 'He showed us tricks with coins and bits of string, and he was always trying to make us play cricket, which we did not wish to do, because we were girls'. The distinguished authoress, Daphne du Maurier, cousin of the Davies boys, in a letter to *The Listener*, writes of playing cricket with him in the garden at Hampstead, so it is apparent that Barrie's inveigling of youngsters for games with a bat and ball was not confined to just one sex.

Cricket, with all its refinements, appealed to Barrie's sense of subtlety. But more than that, it is essentially a game that attracts romantics and nobody ever risked disputation in thus labelling J.M.B. It is a type of escapism for grown-ups that is confined to the young-at-heart; an acceptable form of adult madness in which men can behave like boys and get away with it.

One capricious indoor 'adventure' that Barrie invented for the Davies children and their friends was to write a pantomime which received its sole performance at his Gloucester Road abode in 1901. The specially printed programme announced that 'The Allahakbarrie Cricket Club has the Honour to present for the first and only time on any stage an Entirely Amazing Moral Tale entitled The Greedy Dwarf'. Mr Gerald du Maurier played Allahakbarrie and Miss Mary Contrairy (Barrie's wife) spelt *Allahakbarrie* in the last act.

The amount of effort that Barrie willingly undertook in order to entertain his flock can be seen in a further delightful extravagance later that same year. *The Boy Castaways of Black Lake Island, being a record of the terrible adventures of the brothers Davies in the summer of 1901* was published by J. M. Barrie in the Gloucester Road in only two copies: one of the copies is held by the Beinecke Library at Yale University. In a photograph therein, the two boys are shown lying negligently against a bramble bush and are having 'a last pipe before turning in'. Is one imagining a cricket bat hidden amidst the thick scented primroses on the shores of the Black Lake?

Barrie seized any and every opportunity to play cricket with the brothers Davies. Games in parks and gardens, on beaches and in Campden Hill Square, where the family resided at No. 23 – their importance to Barrie is shown in the many references which occur in his voluminous correspondence. He was overjoyed when the brothers did well at the game at school – four of them, George, Peter, Michael and Nicholas went to Eton, and when George represented the College at Lord's in the annual ding-dong against Harrow, made a handsome score, captured a key wicket and took a brilliant catch, the master of the telling word found difficulty in expressing any that he felt adequate. 'I am greatly delighted and rayther [sic] proud,' wrote Barrie to George eventually.

In an earlier letter, he had been far more constructive. 'This confounded excitement about the XI has rather caught me and I have begun to dream about it. Mix them, curve them, swerve them, break them, and if he still hits it, kick him. I can't think of any better tip . . . I wish I was as good at bowling as at the idiotic thing of flinging rings onto watches . . .'

The younger brother, Michael, was also showing promise as a batsman. Andrew Birkin, in his illuminating book *J. M. Barrie and the Lost Boys*, draws the analogy.

Top left: Authors at Play. J.M.B. and Shan F. Bullock inspecting Frank-fort Moore's motor-cycle. (*Cricket of Today and Yesterday*, Vol. 1 – P.C. Standing). *Top right*: Barrie at the wicket in 1926 during a social visit to Stanway House from the Australian tourists. Encircling slip-field; L to R: M.A. Noble, A. Mailey, H.L. Collins and C.G. Macartney who is looking undecided about acting as wicket-keeper. *Bottom*: Macartney has now made up his mind and is squatting in business-like fashion while Jack Ellis at short leg and Arthur Mailey at fine leg wonder what they are doing there.

The newly-installed Rector of the University of St. Andrew's bowling
to the newly-installed Chancellor, Earl Haig, at the opening of a recreation
ground at Dundee University College in May, 1922.

"THRUMS" HONOURS HER MOST DISTINGUISHED SON

Barrie returns to an old stamping ground in June 1930 when he presents a new pavilion with a camera obscura to the Kirriemuir Club. The match to mark the opening is between West of Scotland and an Allahakbarrie team, for which J.M.B. was nominally 12th man. *Top Left*: Watched by the rival captains, McGregor (Allahakbarries) and Mathieson (West of Scotland) Barrie spins a coin. *Top Right*: Presentation of the Freedom of Kirriemuir. Provost Peacock hands over the casket containing the freedom ticket to the new Burgess.

Sharing a joke with two old friends, Peter Lindsay (holding the bat) and Alex Lowson.

More than a few well-chosen words.

Getting to grips with the willow – Barrie and
Charlie Macartney.

Opposite left: Cricket bat autographed and
presented to Alex Lowson, famous Angus
'demon bowler' of the '70s, by Charles
Macartney, Australian Test cricketer who
scored a century playing for Sir J.M. Barrie's
team, The Allahakbarries, against the West of
Scotland in June 1930. *Opposite right*: To
K.I.D. Mathieson, largest score for West of
Scotland against Allahakbarries C.C. at
Kirriemuir, June 7, 1930 from J.M. Barrie.
Mathieson made 30.

A stroke all of his own making. Macartney wisely taking evasive action.

KIRRIEMUIR CRICKET CLUB.

Season 1930.

BARRIE PAVILION

Opened on JUNE 7th 1930.

PETER LINDSAY. · SIR J.M.BARRIE.   PROVOST H.E.PEACOCK. · A.B.BISSET.

W.SMITH.(Umpire)W.MACARTNEY(Australia)G.MILLS.D.KERMACK. J.SMART. T.BISSET.   A.DICK. G.STRACHAN. A.A.MAILER(Australia) G.STEWART(M⁼)

G.KETTLES.D.STEVENSON(Vice Capt)A.LOWSON.D.M⁼GREGOR(Captain)W.MEARNS. J.R.M⁼GREGOR.

After recounting how 'the dazzling creature' had scored 26 runs in his final prep-school match against Juddy's, Barrie wrote of Michael in *Neil and Tintinnabulum*: 'A rural cricket match in buttercup time with boys at play, seen and heard through the trees; it is surely the loveliest scene in England and the most disarming sound. From the ranks of the unseen dead, forever passing along our country lanes on their eternal journey, the Englishman falls out for a moment to look over the gate of the cricket field and smile. Let Neil's 26 against Juddy's . . . be our last sight of him as a child. He is walking back bat in hand to the pavilion, an old railway carriage. An unearthly glory has swept over the cricket ground. He tries to look unaware of it; you know the expression and the bursting heart . . . (He) gathers up the glory and tacks it over his bed. "The End," as he used to say in his letters. I never knew him quite so well again. He seems henceforth to be running to me on a road that is moving still more rapidly in the opposite direction.'

George Davies, who managed to get a commission in the King's Royal Rifles (so did brother Peter) on the strength of his cricket for Eton, was killed in the First World War and Michael died in a swimming accident (or was it suicide?) just after it. Before hostilities began, Barrie was obviously full of foreboding. In one of his notebooks he writes: 'The Last Cricket Match. One or two days before war declared – my anxiety and premonition – boys gaily playing cricket at Auch, seen from my window – I know they're to suffer – I see them dropping out one by one, fewer and fewer.'

Those ominous thoughts found a voice in *Barbara's Wedding*, produced some thirteen years later at the Savoy Theatre:

The Colonel is in the sitting-room of his country cottage, staring through the open windows at his pretty garden. He is a very old man, and is sometimes bewildered nowadays. You must understand that at the beginning of the play he is just seeing visions of the past. No real people come to him, though he thinks they do. He calls to Dering, the gardener, who is on a ladder, pruning . . .

COLONEL: Where is everyone?

DERING: They're all about, sir. There is a cricket match on at the village green.

COLONEL: Is there?

DERING: If the wind had a bit of south in it you could hear their voices. You were a bit of a nailer at cricket yourself, sir.

(The Colonel sees himself standing up to fast ones. He is gleeful over his reminiscences.)

COLONEL: Ninety-nine against Mallowfield, and then bowled off my pads. Biggest score I ever made. Mallowfield wanted to add one to make it the hundred, but I wouldn't let them. I was pretty good at steering them through the slips, Dering! Do you remember my late cut? It didn't matter where point stood, I got past him. You used to stand at point, Dering.

DERING: That was my grandfather, sir. If he was to be believed, he used to snap you regular at point.

(The Colonel is crestfallen, but he has a disarming smile.)

COLONEL: Did he? I dare say he did. I can't play now, but I like to watch it still. (He becomes troubled again) Dering, there's no cricket on the green to-day. I have been down to look. I don't understand it, Dering. When I got there the green was all dotted with them. But as I watched them they began to go away, one and two at a time; they weren't given out, you know, they went as if they had been called away. Some of the little shavers stayed on – and then they went off, as if they had been called away too. The stumps were left lying about. Why is it?

DERING: It's just fancy, sir. I saw Master Will oiling his bat yesterday.

COLONEL (avidly): Did you? I should have liked to see that. I have often oiled their bats for them. Careless lads, they always forget.

Barrie was eventually to see Nico emulate his brother George and turn out for Eton against Harrow at Lord's, but his hope that all four of his own Etonians would play in the match had been shattered by the exigencies of war and the fell hand of Fate.

[7]

CRICKET AT STANWAY

S TANWAY, the country home of Lord and Lady Wemyss, parents to his
secretary, Cynthia Asquith, was only five miles from Broadway,
where Barrie had so often led the inimitable Allahakbarries to re-
sounding defeat. After the First World War, the cloistered, gabled six-
teenth-century house with its Jacobean garden front and Inigo Jones
gatehouse became a kind of second home to Barrie and though ostensibly
always a visitor, he was, in a blurred and undefined way, a kind of host to the
other friends who had been invited.

'At Stanway, where for thirteen years in succession Barrie spent August
in a house packed with a wonderful variety of guests, he played with
contagious ardour in countless after-tea matches between picked-up sides of
children, village boys, nursery-maids and any docile members of the house
party.' The keenest of all the players was Millie, the nursery-maid. No other
fielder took such risks to keep runs down as this intrepid girl, who seldom
used her hands but would intercept any ball with some portion or other of
her anatomy.

Barrie: Why didn't you stop that ball with your hand, Millie, instead of with
    your head?

Millie: My head seemed to come more handy, Sir.

Cynthia Asquith continues:

I still have a vivid picture of his short legs frenziedly running out an
equally engaging but less zealous cricketer, the six-foot seven-long
professor, Sir Walter Raleigh. These two were the most entrancingly
ill-matched pair of batsmen it has ever been my pleasure to see . . . –
the bails are off at *both* ends! And how thankful the batsmen were to
fling themselves panting onto the grass, for they were running their

fifth run, and the laces of both Barrie's shoes had come untied. It mustn't be supposed that either the long or the short batsman had had the satisfaction of making a good hit, but a ball swiped at by 'The Professor', and missed, had slipped through the butter-fingers, first of the wicket-keeper (aged six) and then of the long-stop (aged four) who, when at long last she overtook the ball, firmly sat down upon it and refused to yield it up.

At Stanway, too, Barrie delighted to watch the dramas and humours of village cricket. Saturday after Saturday would find him perched, pipe in hand, on the most uncompromisingly hard wooden bench, scrutinising every movement of the game and congratulating or commiserating each out-coming batsman. In gratitude for many hours of enjoyment, he presented the Stanway Cricket Club with a fine pavilion. Until then a railway carriage (3rd class) had done duty. It was a characteristic irony of a kind with which he was well acquainted that his generous gift should rather spoil the lovely village cricket ground for himself. Perhaps it made it seem too like Lord's. But it was much appreciated by the residents and their visitors.

Apparently, Barrie specially enjoyed the innings of Harry Last, the corduroyed gamekeeper, who emulated his name by going in at number eleven. (Distant shades of Jemmy Clinker, the local cobbler and a great cricketer in 'The Captain of the School' from *A Holiday in Bed*.) Last had a reckless, dashing, hit-or-miss style which ensured either a lively ten minutes or an early tea.

The scoring at the ground was decidedly idiosyncratic. The white figures on square pieces of black tin were frequently put in the wrong order. A puzzled onlooker might read:

Runs	32
Wickets	7
Last Man	130

Not that it seemed to make that much difference to the result.

Cricket dances, cricket charades, games of golf-croquet, shuffleboard and chucking stamps to stick on the ceiling all helped to make the weeks at Stanway a powerful attraction for Barrie. He also spent time there during the Christmas holidays of the Wemyss grandchildren and wrote special plays for them to perform, 'Where was Simon?' and 'The Wheel'. But it was at the times when a cricketing fraternity were in residence, or visiting, that he was at his happiest.

Most of the Eton XI came one year and Barrie listened with amusement to their faltering attempts at speech-making after the last dinner. Some of them came up to him afterwards and asked for a rating. With droll perversity, Barrie awarded highest marks to the worst performers.

Another year a few of the Australian touring side, who were appearing at Cheltenham, paid a visit. Warwick Armstrong, Jack Gregory and Arthur Mailey played cricket with the children and signed Cynthia Asquith's son's bat, much to his annoyance. 'Mother, isn't there any writing paper in the house? Why did you let all those men spoil my beautiful new bat?'

During 1926, the entire Australian XI turned up and stayed for lunch, tea and dinner. Collins, Mailey and Macartney decided to spend the night. Macartney needed a little persuasion to do so because he said he had a long letter to finish to his wife. Barrie promised to write the letter and as a way of saying thank you Macartney allowed himself to be clean bowled by the Allahakbarrie captain the next morning.

Two years before, Barrie had exceeded even those dizzy heights. In a game in the village he had performed the hat trick. Is it too unkind to suggest that it might possibly have happened with perhaps just a little help from his friends . . . ?

[8]

ROUND AND ABOUT BARRIE

IT is not to be wondered at that Barrie was never short of *bon* and less than *bon mots* on his contemporaries. Nor were they on him.

W. G. Grace in his *Cricketing Reminiscences:*

Mr J. M. Barrie, the Scotch novelist – who is an ardent cricketer and when playing for the Authors against the Press at Lord's is said to have fielded 'brilliantly with his hands in his pockets' – tells a story of a man notable for his pedantry who was batting one day when Mr Barrie was wicket-keeping. 'If I strike the ball with even the slightest degree of impulse,' remarked the batsman, addressing the wicket-keeper, 'I shall immediately commence running with considerable velocity.' There was no occasion (adds Mr Barrie naively) for him to commence.

Cricketing companion E. V. Lucas thought that of all the imaginative writers of his time, Barrie looked most like his work.

Barrie on 'The Cricket Match' by Hugh de Selincourt:

. . . the best that has ever been written about cricket or any other game.

'I had a great knowledge of the game except in the actual knowledge of the playing thereof.'

William Kent who wrote the biography of *John Burns, Labour's Lost Leader*, relates how Burns, who was a mighty striker of the ball, told him of an occasion when Barrie, in top hat and hansom cab, came to Battersea Park with a view to some practice. At the time Burns was at the wicket and knocking the bowling of some local boys all over the place.

The fusillade of leather from his shots was so terrific that Barrie, who had apparently not yet qualified to deliver the St Andrews lecture on courage, decided on a hasty retreat, and left the park in the same cab wherein he went.

Neville Cardus came to know Barrie through cricket. He wrote to him complaining of alterations to the original text of *Peter Pan*. Barrie replied: 'I am elated to hear that you spend your sixpences on P. Pan and that you know when bits of him fall off. I expect the explanation is that the author is a little like Macartney and tires of seeing himself always making the same strokes . . .' Cardus wrote that Barrie 'not only admired Charles Macartney, most brilliant of all Australian batsmen with the single exception of Victor Trumper; he actually envied him. "He can do all that he wants to do," was his significant tribute.'

Barrie once invited Cardus to his flat in Adelphi Terrace. Cardus had just come from Lord's and had hardly entered the door when Barrie asked: 'How did Root bowl today? I've just read the close of play score.' Cardus reminded him that he had once been a working journalist himself, so he would see the point of waiting till tomorrow morning to read his report in the paper.

A few weeks later, they met at Lord's in front of the old Tavern. Cardus asked Barrie if he would like to come and sit with him in the Pavilion. 'No,' he replied, 'I like to stand here amongst the crowd. So many things happen to you here at Lord's. It's astonishing the number of people you meet who know you. Only five minutes ago, a perfect stranger, wearing a cloth cap and a spotted handkerchief round his neck, came out of the Tavern, put down his can of beer, patted me on the shoulder and said "Ello George!"'

In his *Autobiography*, Cardus recalls another visit to Lord's one morning in the company of Barrie. 'We sat at right angles to the wicket, a most unprofessional place for me because I like to see the spin. But Barrie preferred the stand over the Tavern at Lord's near the dining-room; I think he imagined he was taking me to a cricket match as though I were one of his adopted grown-up children; he asked me after we had sat in the sun an hour or so whether I would like an ice-cream. Also he asked me what I thought of J. W. Hearne as a bowler: "I mean do you call him – as an expert – fast or

[135]

slow?" J. W. Hearne was a slow leg-break bowler, and I replied: "Slow of course; in fact, very slow." Barrie meditated for a while, took another look at Hearne's bowling and said: "For my part I should say he's pretty fast." Here followed a pause for more meditation, then he added: "You must come down to Stanway and watch me. I can bowl so slow that if I don't like a ball I can run after it and bring it back." He used this remark at a speech to the Australian team later on; he never wasted a word. Seldom could I get him to talk about anything except cricket.'

Barrie was on one of his many visits to Lord's when a young boy asked him to sign his autograph book. He noticed the pages were of different colours and the boy added quickly: 'Please sir, don't sign on a pink page.' 'Why?' queried Barrie. 'Because pink pages are reserved for Test Match cricketers only,' replied the boy. Barrie signed on a blue page and then was considerably taken aback when a moment later the Archbishop of Canterbury came up and signed on a pink one.

Barrie quote: 'I saw "Plum" Warner bat, I think, twice. On the first occasion he made one run; on the second he was not quite so successful.'

Barrie quote: 'Woolley whispered to the ball, which at once hastened to the boundary just to please him.'

Once Barrie asked who was the slowest bowler in first-class cricket. 'Cranfield of Somerset' was the answer. Barrie mused that he himself was 'half as fast as Cranfield'.

One day in Kent, the opposition included two county bowlers. When Barrie's turn came to bat he turned to a friend and handed him the pipe he had been smoking. 'Will you hold this?' he asked. The pipe was still in when Barrie returned.

Was it Bernard Darwin who wrote:

. . . and devotee, Sir J. M. Barrie, had, as I suppose, seen little cricket at Kirriemuir, was, by all accounts, a wholly inconsiderable player. Generally speaking, the game seems to make a strong appeal to literary personalities, perhaps because they appreciate all its romantic qualities, whether it is played on Broadway or at Trent Bridge.

Conan Doyle of JMB:

Barrie, about whom there is nothing small except his body . . .

Barrie was no novice. He bowled an insidious left-hand good-length ball coming from leg which was always likely to get a wicket.

Denis Mackail on Barrie as a cricketer:

As for his own prowess – if that is the right word for it – one might tabulate it in some such manner as this. He knew everything about the theory of cricket, and could have chosen and directed the best team in the world. His slow, left-handed bowling – possibly the slowest that has yet been seen – was subtle, accurate, and maddeningly effective. His right-handed batting – for in games where both arms are employed he was always a right-hander – was almost uniformly unsuccessful. But perhaps his greatest distinction was the astounding courage with which he faced the fastest or most incalculable ball. For in those matches, as can well be imagined, it might appear from anywhere or at any velocity, and imperil any part of one's person. He never flinched. He hardly troubled to dodge. His calm was spectacular, and no violent or unexpected blow was ever seen to disturb it. It was the others who gasped, yelled, or shuddered, but never Barrie. Indomitable; there can be no other epithet to sum up the cricketing spirit in that small and fragile frame.

In a letter to Andrew Birkin, Nico Davies recalled J.M.B. bowling to him between two wooden chairs in Campden Hill Square and also another occasion:

'One of my favourite memories is of him telling me of some biggish dinner given . . . at the Oval, I think – to the Australians, maybe by Surrey . . . Uncle Jim made one of his marvellous speeches and when he'd finished the Australian captain, Woodfull, said: "And now Gentlemen, the speaker to whom we have all *really* been looking forward – ANDY SANDHAM!"'

[137]

[9]

COPIOUS CORRESPONDENCE

BARRIE held the view, or said he did, that all correspondence should be destroyed. Fortunately, the recipients of his amusing and intimate epistles, written in his illegible, cramped hand, felt otherwise or neglected to do so. Viola Meynell performed a singular service for posterity when she collected the letters of JMB for publication by Peter Davies, who was forever haunted by the tag 'Peter Pan'.

Barrie's letters show him in his most characteristic poses without the shyness that often inhibited the spoken word. As is to be expected, cricket is often on the agenda. We find references to Macartney and the Australians; to Percival Lucas (E.V.'s brother), one of Barrie's cricketing brethren, killed in the First World War; to a cricketer's feeling when he goes in to bat; to conversations with Neville Cardus; to how he (Barrie) used to walk three miles to watch matches at Glamis. We also find many comments about the Davies boys' cricketing achievements and about watching matches; concern expressed for Cynthia Asquith's young son Michael: 'I decided not to get a cricket ball for M. as the tennis one is safer'; and an autobiographical note: 'At my school we used to play another school at cricket, and they worried us by playing the same boy in flannels for the 1st XI and in knickerbockers for the 2nd and in a kilt for the 3rd. We could never quite prove it but he was a great thorn in our side.'

An interesting letter of Barrie's was to fellow author, H. G. Wells:

My dear Wells

Certain Personal Matters of my own have got in the way of my thanking you for the copy of your book [*Certain Personal Matters*] which I do very heartily. I'm glad you collected these papers for many of them are long lost friends of mine, and furthermore the

'Veteran Cricketer' which is new strikes me of a heap. Not by its merit (pooh) but because I have you now; – you have a secret desire to spank them to leg and lift beauties to the off, and you probably can't, and so you are qualified for my cricket team. Elected whether you grumble or not.

Nine months later, in the summer of '98, he was in touch again:

Are you coming to my cricket match? It takes place on Saturday next the 11th at Broadway, Worcestershire, against a team of artists, etc got up by Mrs de Navarro (Mary Anderson that was). We had a great time last year, and none of us can play. We are going down the previous day, for which she has arranged sports etc of a wild nature, a supper also at which there are great doings. Cricket on Saturday, return on Sunday. Our train leaves Paddington Friday morning at 9.50. Book second class to Evesham and bring evening dress.

Where cricket was concerned, Barrie could be very persuasive. For a game against Shere, he made H. B. Marriott Watson, the New Zealand journalist, an offer he couldn't refuse:

My dear Watson

Let us say June 18, as that is the date they prefer and I shall try to get an XI for that day. The main fun of the thing, not to speak of the sentiment, would lie in their being the old team as much as possible, and the same with ours. I count upon yourself and will try to get Gilmour, Reid and Partridge – a really weak team.

The English public school image was something of which Barrie was constantly and nigglingly aware. He was partly intrigued by its manifestations, partly resentful and reluctantly admiring of them. In 1920, he wrote to Cynthia Asquith:

[139]

I went with N. [Nicholas] to the Lord's match. 15,000 tall hats – one cad hat (mine); 15,000 stiff collars, canes, shiny faces – one soft collar, cudgel, dreary face (mine). The ladies comparatively drab fearing rain but the gents superb, colossal, sleek, lovely. All with such a pleased smile. Why? Because they know they had the Eton something or the Harrow something. They bestowed the something on each other, exchanged with each other as the likes of me exchange the time of day. I felt I was nearer to grasping what the something is than ever before. It is a sleek happiness that comes of a shininess which only Eton (or Harrow) can impart. This makes you 'play the game' as the damned can't do it; it gives you manners because you know in your heart that nothing really matters so long as you shine with that sleek happiness. The nearest thing to it must be boot polish. Does this bore you? Am I at it again?

Ten years later, he wrote to his secretary once more, when she was vacationing in Venice:

There were some scraps in papers about the cricket dinner of Monday but I think it was meant to be private. I had a letter from Simon today and mean to rub it into him that I sat beside Woodfull and had talks with Bradman, Chapman, Ranji, etc. Good effect when I said of Bradman that I was very sorry for him as I couldn't doubt that he had meant to do better [Bradman had just made a record number of Test-match centuries]. I also got in a local touch by saying that I hoped Woodfull felt he ought to give a handful of the Ashes to Gloucestershire. A sad thing that Faulkner the greatest of South African cricketers who was there was found dead this morning with the gas on.

Barrie also corresponded with Lady Cynthia's mother and thanked her for a stay at Stanway:

As for the tithe barn I revelled in it until I had to take the Australian team over it one at a time, and by the time I escorted the tenth man

[140]

through it I wished it had been destroyed by William the Conqueror (who by the way I told them had been shown over it just as they were, and probably made the same remarks. They were so dazed that I fancy they thought it was I who showed him over it, and I am beginning to think that myself).

A missive that Barrie sent to Lady Mary Strickland contains barely disguised pathos and loneliness:

It is very nice of you to remember me for the Eton and Harrow match, but flown away are now all the birds and I suppose I shall no more grace that festive scene. Caught, bowled and run out for ever.

Barrie enjoyed cricketing allusions. Referring to the ill-fated musical *Jane Annie*, he wrote:

'Jane Annie' was a dreadful failure. I had undertaken to do it '*off my own bat*' for the D'Oyly Carte's, and went into hiding to escape it, was discovered and brought back and allowed to introduce a collaborator, who was Doyle.

Perhaps the most voluminous correspondence was between Barrie and his long-standing friend, the elusive and unpresuming writer of school stories, Charles Turley Smith. 'Dear Turley' lived in Cornwall and for many years Barrie used to send lengthy telegrams with the stop-press news from Lord's or the Oval, so that his friend should know the latest position before the information could be gleaned from the newspapers. Barrie deliberately interlaced facetious and melodramatic comment with sober fact. 'Dreadful delay. Fielding superb. So and so hurriedly learning to bowl. Score XXX.' Barrie never quite forgave the BBC for the introduction of wireless, which meant that Turley knew the score as soon as he did. The ether had no effect though on their cricket confederacy. The self-appointed Selection Committee of two carried on their correspondence with childish delight. Turley kept all Barrie's letters:

4 July 1913

The test match had its features – Hobbs, Rhodes, Macartney. But—
was dreadful beyond words, he was just a stick shoving the ball back.
My best memory is Barnes bowling. He took no wickets but it was
the most 'classic' sight I have seen since Richardson. What do I mean
by classic? Well thus I feel the Greeks would have bowled.

16 September 1924

The great news (which I hope will leave you breathless for a space) is
that three weeks or less ago I played in one of Nicholas's matches at
Stanway. Even that is news as I have not played anywhere since
before the war. But it is not the astounding news. The Stanway XI
(which has been quite swagger this year) were our opponents and on
being put on to bowl I did the Hat Trick in my fourth over, one of my
victims being the cock of the walk. One bowled, two stumped,
Bridgeman being the stumps. What a glory for you and all Allahakbarries. I ought to be one of the Big Five in *Wisden*. In the same
match Worthington (who was 12th man for Eton in Nico's year)
made 139 not out, including about eight sixes and 16 fours. No, I am
not going to America, but obviously I ought to be packing for
Australia.

1 October 1925

I consider that in your choice of test teams Champain and you cover
yourselves with ignominy, though *you* may be dragged out while *he* is
sunk from sight. As 'One who knows' (my name in this matter) there
are four certainties, Hobbs, Sutcliffe, Tate, Macaulay. He omits
Sutcliffe altogether, and you gingerly include him at the end. The
man who stood out beyond all in Australia in the tests. Why have you
this ill-will to him? What is behind it?

We must have an amateur captain I suppose, so I grant you Carr.
That is all the 'certs'. Strudwick may still be the best wicket-keeper. I
give you Holmes, Woolley and Kilner – not Fender nor Sandham
(Fender courageous but he couldn't get those blokes out and
Sandham doesn't seem to have Test qualities.) I hanker after
Hammond or Hallows, but we must have two bowlers – chosen from
Larwood, Root, Parker.

This knocks out Hendren and Hearne, as having proved themselves not great Test men, but it only *guesses* their substitutes *may* be better.

On paper we can't make a superior team to the Test XI that were in Australia except for one man, Macaulay, who certainly adds something definite. I feel like risking Larwood (especially if he changes his name to Harwood – must have another H.).

(To be continued.)   The only One Who Knows

                                                                    1 April 1926
Have you seen the articles on the Tests that are appearing in papers by Clem Hill and Noble? Clement has a judicious and pleasant pen but Noble boundereth a bit, and maketh it more necessary that we should disturb the invader. If our 'tail' was one that lashed we might make some use of it. They are trusting a lot to that tail, and we must admit that the kangaroo hath it not. I have agreed to go to a press luncheon to them a day or two after they arrive, and if possible will cast the Evil Eye upon them. I see Parkin has said that if Mailey and Grimmett were in League Cricket here they would never be heard of. This is the stuff to give them. I expect it is not so far from the truth too. The problem is how to get them promptly into League cricket, and to find Gregory already there. This is all intended to encourage your hopes. Since reading Noble I have a fine confidence that we shall pull it off. Oxford should recover now that Holmes has passed his exam. How he got that wicket deponent knoweth not. He should now be able to open any oyster.

                                                                    8 June 1926
That seems unfair of you to have an extra rib, but not only that, to keep it up your sleeve as it is apparently in your arm. Your bowling arm? If so you might lend it to Tate. Evidently it is no use to you and I do hope the medicine men will dispose of its power for harm. I am very glad Mrs Millet is so much better. Please, my love to her. I went yesterday to England v. The Rest and was very bored. Hobbs had no gaiety, but, my word, he played like a true master of the game and his placing made all others comparatively clodpoles. They seemed nearly all to be paralysed. Duleep's catch was a line of poetry tho'.

[143]

Larwood I expect will be a swell ere long. I suppose Root will play instead of Allen. It will be quaint if the rest win. High time Carr proved his choice.

24 July 1926

I hope you are feeling pretty right again, though I am none so sure and would like a bill of your health. I thought there had been Test cricket, as it has been a good day here until evening. What is needed is not more time for matches but a fleet of aeroplanes to rush the combatants about England in search of a dry spot where they could alight and toss at once. I conclude from the composition of the English XI that the idea was for a draw, leaving the final match to decide. It should then be composed of the eleven who can stick in longest waiting for the loose ball. I was hoping Carr would win the toss to-day and put the Australians in again – a pretty sure way to getting into *Wisden* for ever.

I am going to Stanway about August 4 for a month and as the Australians are to be playing Glo'ster at Cheltenham, 7, 9 and 10th, several of them will probably be staying with us and they'll all come over on Sunday. Does not this tempt you to come for a few days? I wish it would.

7 March 1927

Wisden's has arrived and was received with 21 guns, if that is the correct number for a royal reception. He is now playing a triangle match here with Trollope and Winston's 'How I won the War,' and the one who has done best for the day is the one I take to bed with me. There is good scoring going on all round and so far no one is out.

2 March 1930

Avaunt. This is addressed to myself for not having thanked you for *Wisden* ere this. You must take as compliment however that if I'd seen it in a shop window before it reached me I'd have sent you promptly enough a letter of remonstrance. It now makes a nice solid weapon for throwing at stone-wallers. Though their test team is so much younger than ours they are probably still slower.

14 September 1930

Yes, rather, I went to see *The Left Hander*, it has a special appeal to me now that I write left handed and always bowled left as you have no doubt good cause to remember though I don't believe you do. We talked those old days over again at the Navarros the other day, and there were several priests there with whom I made an unintentional hit by saying (perhaps brazenly) that I had once made two fours and a five, and I found afterwards that they thought I said I had made 245 and now are telling everyone about my prowess, so when next you sit between two priests do be careful and don't give me away.

That dinner with the Australians was quite enjoyable and I said in my remarks that I hoped when Woodfull was sitting in his cabin on the way home nursing the Ashes he sometimes would wonder whether he should not have given a handful of them to Gloucestershire. I have since had a letter from Bradman asking me to write a preface to his forthcoming book but am not doing it. Thus you see I now move in highish circles.

19 February 1931

Wisden's has at last come and I sat far into last night with him, which is my best thanks for him – or if there are better I send them also. I gather that you are now a bit better, and for that, after all, I thank you still more. I seem fairly right myself too. As for SA cricket, it seems plain that we need to send our best possible elevens there, and a numerous reserve as they get so wounded. Peebles and Voce seem to promise well for the future. I feel sorry for Chapman who has everything in his favour except the score-sheet.

6 May 1931

If you had not that wireless to spoil my cricket messages I'd have felt impelled to send you a telegram with the result of Glos'ter v. Surrey. Lyon is a nailor for audacious cricket and will evidently compel some other counties to follow suit. Some day he will start with the second innings. This young Hardstuff at 17 must look on Bradman as quite an old chap.

20 September 1931

Your team is a happier subject, and I agree with you that all you mention should cross the seas, if Hobbs be willing. I would keep

[145]

Fassimond for 2nd wicket-keeper and put Ames first. The extra people should perhaps be Robins, Peebles, Bowes and I have a hankering after Chapman as probably a better captain than Jardine – heartier and more able to cheer his men. Three fast bowlers is probably wrong for Austr. wickets, but I don't think Robins and Peebles can be left out. Did I tell you of my being at the Canterbury week and hobnobbing with the Kent and Somerset men? The Somerset hard hitter whose name I forget for the moment had only one over, as follows – 1 (really a miss) 6 (into a wood), 6 (into the town) 0 (but it was nearly 12), 6 (into the cathedral), and next bowled neck and crop by Freeman. If budgets could only be balanced in this way!

10 October 1931

Yes, Earle was the man I saw smiting them. I forget if I told you of a schoolboy at Stanway who asked me to write my name in his autograph book. It had various coloured pages and he told me to write on a yellow one. Afterwards I found the book on a table and found written in it 'Pink pages specially reserved for cricketers only.' Oh, my pharynx, O, my larynx!

4 December 1932

What warfare in Australia! We have certainly made a big start but I think people are far too confident in looking on the match as already won against such stout opponents and the weather and the 4th innings. Larwood's three wickets after lunch was in the grand style and I hope to have good news for you to-morrow. Ditto about McCabe. I sent him a cable: 'Glorious performance by the night-lights-boy' – a reference to my having told him here that he was so young I understood he could not sleep without a night-light. I think both teams made a mistake in not having an extra bowler. The A's should have included Ironmonger. It all seems mysterious about Bradman and sad too. Whatever it is it may have been his reason for all that earlier correspondence about other engagements. Evidently several of their best funk Larwood, but they will reconstruct their team if necessary in their game way and learn how to deal with such bowling. In the meantime Jardine seems to be very capable and it's

[146]

funny about his cap. I think he should remove Larwood entirely for tests, and Voce as much as possible. That curious treatment of the ground to spoil shock tactics may have spoilt Allen – and also the fuss about his boots. Hendren says he never disturbed the ground here. I am assuming that our bowling is all legitimate. Armstrong writes unpleasantly about it, but that does not move me. What a team we could have had with Duleep and Robins and another bowler!

5 August 1934

I haven't actually seen any cricket but follow the movements in the press. I don't think you will be able to wangle Robins into your side for the Test, but the bowling of Allen to-day should give them to think. Odd about Hammond who after all is our best. Woodfull (take note) is coming out strong again. Bradman has been staying at my surgeon, Shields's, cottage in the Burnham Beeches. I saw a long letter from him the other day which was one of the nicest and warmest I have ever seen from a young man.

21 March 1935

Wisden's came all right, and many thanks to you. I, also, find I can't go through it with the zest of yore nor do I thrill over our rather lamentable experiences against Headley, Constantine and Co. Very sorry surely that Wyatt had his skull cracked, but alas again.

13 October 1936

You seem to be having a bad time in bed with your throat and I am very sorry. I cough away interminably but somehow the throat seems to be listless about it, and I am in fair fettle. I'll be occupied a bit now with the resumed rehearsals of my play. [*The Boy David*]

If the Rest has beaten the 1st 11 in Australia to-day it will be an excess of the grotesque like the counties here against the Indians. I think two equal teams (outside the glorious uncertainty) for the tests would be as they stand except that Bradman plays for Britain and Hammond for Australia. They are undoubtedly the two champions but B. is the certainty and if we gave him 150 not to play (for two innings) it would be quite worth our while. We seem weakest in our two opening batsmen, whoever they turn out to be. Our best XI

[147]

might have batsmen, all but the last man, either Farnes or Copson, who are no good with the bat nor on the field. Or we could play neither of them and have a complete batting and fielding side. What does your throat think of that?

18 March 1937

Just a line to thank you for *Wisden*'s and to report progress. The Sciatica, etc, are still going pretty grim at times, but at other hours I feel well and am getting a lot of 'treatment', and at times indeed there are about as many hot water bottles in my bed as runs on an English test score sheet.

Other letters to Turley contained lines such as 'judging by results that "smaller ball" is what the Allahakbarries needed throughout their career' and 'I wish cricketers would put on a few extra garments and take to the field if only in the interests of newspaper-readers.' What would Barrie have thought of the modern streaker, I wonder?

In 1906, J.M.B. received a letter from Alfred D. Taylor enquiring if it were possible to acquire a copy of the 1899 Allahakbarrie booklet. Taylor was putting the finishing touches to his *Catalogue of Cricket Literature* and was understandably anxious to make it as comprehensive as he could. Barrie replied: 'The pamphlet you mention is of no value. As it is strictly private you must forgive me if I do not send you a copy.'

Probably in Barrie's mind at that moment was the thought that he did not want to regenerate the interest of the press in the doings of the Allahakbarries. The publicity surrounding the Broadway matches had caused them to seek quieter pastures a few years later and he had no wish to be forced to find further new venues. As to his observation that the 'pamphlet is of no value', he would undoubtedly be astounded to hear of present-day estimates close to four figures.

Another letter of Barrie's that has cricket associations was to a William Yeaman of Edinburgh and enclosed with it was a cheque, to help restore the fortunes of Alexander Haggart, a boyhood friend in Kirriemuir who had taught Barrie how to hold a bat.

He was the soul of generosity when it came to helping those less fortunate than himself. In 1905, he joined with several other literary men of distinction, Andrew Lang, Conan Doyle, E. V. Lucas and also E. W. Hornung, in starting a fund for the three Misses Nyren, granddaughters of John Nyren (of *Young Cricketers' Tutor* fame), whose boarding house in Folkestone had hit hard times. Barrie set the ball rolling with £20.

Undoubtedly, Barrie's most publicised letter was the one, or was it two, that he sent to *The Times* in 1930. The mini-saga started when an unnamed correspondent wrote to the paper lamenting the end of his playing days:

A LAST INNINGS
The Brigadier's Exit
(from a Correspondent)

There comes a time when a man begins to realize that his cricket days are over. The thing first began to dawn on me when I noticed that the captain of the side, whenever he started to set his fielders, invariably began by saying, 'General, will you go point?' So I decided to chuck it; but I would go down with colours flying; I would get up a side, I would captain it, I would play a captain's innings, and then I would retire 'to make room for younger men'. Accordingly I decided to challenge one of the battalions of the brigade to a match. It gratefully accepted the honour. What else could it do? And when the great day came I had collected a very useful side, including several of the star turns of the garrison. It was a bright, sunny day; rather warm perhaps; but this is to be expected at the beginning of the hot weather in India.

I made an initial error of a kind a captain should never make: I lost the toss. The battalion batted first. It made 101 runs, about 18 of which were the result of my non-bending. I also missed catching the best batsman before he had scored; he then proceeded to make 37. I thought it a difficult catch, and there were sympathetic remarks of 'hard luck' from two or three soldiers who were included in my side; but from a chance remark from a subaltern which I happened to overhear later on, my opinion as to the difficulty of the catch was not shared by some of my side.

We started well. Fifty was up on the board before a wicket had fallen. With the abnegation of the great man, I had put myself in last, and it now looked as if I should not get an innings at all. But a new bowler was put on, one of the last draft just out from home, who was

[149]

reported to be useful. He clean bowled two of my best bats in his first over and three more in his next. Five for 53. Then we pulled ourselves together and the score laboriously mounted up. But wickets continued to fall. We reached 100, but the ninth wicket fell next ball. Two runs to get to win and one wicket to fall, and I was that wicket. I confess my heart bumped; but here was the chance I had asked for – the captain's innings.

As I strode out into the bright light which beats upon a batsman in India my courage returned. At any rate, I felt, I looked the part. I was wearing a dazzlingly white polo helmet: I remembered that at the time of purchase I resented paying £3 for this hat; now I felt that it was worth it. My shirt was a wonderful creation cut short above elbows and made of some patent stuff full of small holes. My trousers were a dream of creaminess and creases. My socks were – (but no one could see them, so that was all right). My boots were simply 'It'. I had borrowed pads and gloves, but not before I had noted they were of the best make; the gloves were covered with a sort of Chevaux-de-frise of black indiarubber and had the right military touch. My borrowed bat had some sticking-plaster in the correct place and the autograph of a famous cricketer and about umpteen crosses on its face; these, for some reason, suddenly reminded me of the marks put at the end of most of the soldiers' letters which I had to censor in France years ago.

I reached the wicket. The umpire obligingly told me my bat was covering middle and leg. Taking the lump of chalk from behind the wicket, I drew a beautiful straight line along the coconut matting from the bat to the wicket. At any rate my hand was steady. I had a look round at the position of the fielders. I noticed with satisfaction that there was no one on the boundary between short-leg and mid-on; that is my favourite place for a drive in the air, which I confess, however, has many times caused my downfall. One run to tie, two to win. I faced the bowler. I felt my stance was all that it should be, and I did not forget to raise my left toe from the ground. The bowler was the successful last-drafter; but what matter? A two is an easy thing to get. The last-drafter took a longish run and then flung the ball at me. Long before the ball left his hand I had quite decided that whatever sort of ball it was, it was to go to my favourite place on the boundary.

The ball hit the bat. At such moments thoughts come like a flash; my flash was a hope that somebody in the crowd of spectators had one of those long-distance high-velocity cameras which photograph cricketers in action; this great shot of mine, I felt, was one which should be recorded. Then an extraordinary thing happened. The ball was not taking its proper course to the boundary; it was going slowly, but beautifully straight, direct to mid-on. Unless anything unforeseen happened to it, it would hit him full in the stomach. Alas! Something did happen to it. The fielder, no doubt as self-protection, put his hands in the course of the ball. The ball stayed in his hands. I was out. The match was lost.

Speechless, I walked back to the tent, accompanied by the batsman from the other end. We were received with respectful cheers; at least I think they were cheers. I sat down and took off my armour. The soldier audience was moving away behind the tent. I heard a man say, ''Bout time Brigadier give oop cricket'. He has done so.

Surely, such a moving letter could not but help appeal to the sensibilities of a man like Barrie. Of course, it did:

CRICKETERS ALL
Sir James Barrie to The Brigadier
An Invitation to Dinner
To the Editor of *The Times*

30 April 1930

Sir,
Now that May and the Australians are upon us is it permissible, for just this once, to make use of *The Times* as a means of inviting an attractive man to dinner? I don't know him, but he is a Brigadier and he says in *The Times* of to-day that he realizes his cricketing days are over; surely this is a combination that will melt even your stubborn heart. In this hope I ask you to forward my invitation to him, and to take note that I leave it open as a guarantee of good faith.

Dear Brigadier, Though I don't know you I wish I did, and that is the only excuse I can offer for my presumption in begging you to dine with me at any time or place that is seemly to you. I have already known one brigadier, which makes me the more desirous to know another, but it is to-day's confession in *The Times* about your last cricket exploit that makes me long to see you sitting opposite me at a table for two. This, however, can create no similar craving in you, and so I hasten to offer you my credentials.

Though I am not a brigadier (through no fault of my own) I, too, can look back upon days when I led my men into the tented field, and to the last match of all when I performed so differently from you that ordinary civility prevents my stating at this early period of our acquaintance what I did, though it may come out at our little dinner. As cricket teaches most things and being a brigadier must teach the rest, you will, I am sure, pardon me for pointing out that on the great occasion you made a regrettable mistake in going in last. I gather indeed (reluctantly) that it was your practice to be tenth man or so, for the same reason that always made me go in first. Modesty, of course, was at the root of it in both cases, but I had evidently thought the matter out more elaborately than you. You were no doubt influenced by the reflection that with a little luck you might carry out your bat, though you should have known (I say it with all deference) that when the ninth wicket falls there are always four more balls to that over. Furthermore, you were playing for the glory of the moment when you should have been thinking of posterity. No one seeing you go in last, or hearing that you go in last, or noticing in *The Times* that you went in last, will ever credit you with being a batsman, not even if you get into double figures. Now, having thought the matter out profoundly, I always as captain went in first. This did not deceive the onlookers, and still less my side, as to my prowess, but I was intentionally playing a waiting game. Readers of the local weekly seeing that I opened the innings, same as Hobbs does, took for granted that I was an accomplished bat who on this occasion happened to be 'unfortunate'. I never got into *The Times*, but I became vaguely known to its readers as a man who went in first and all the rest followed. If I had been you in your last match, instead of going in last I would have gone in first. The result of the match would have been the same, but very likely the reporters (hoodwinked) would have said it was owing to my not making my usual stand.

The things we can talk about if you will only come to dinner! The Australians, for instance. I must admit that I have a leaning to them, being such a young side and having, all the time they are batting or holding out their hands for a catch, to remember the 67 rules they have sworn not to break about wives and autographs. This puts me into an awkward position, which I shall ask your opinion of at our dinner, and is briefly this. I daresay when you were a captain (I mean a real captain, not a military one) you had my experience about tossing? The opposing captain, after looking me over, always told me to toss, and he called 'The Bird', and then, whether the coin came down head or tail, he said, 'The Bird it is; we shall go in.' I often felt there was something wrong about this, but could never quite see what it was. Now do you think that, as the Australians are such a young side and have so many things to remember, I would be justified in dropping a line to Mr Woodfull, saying that the toss is very important, and putting him up to calling 'The Bird'?

Another thing, ought I to give him or Mr Hornibrook a tip about slow left-hand bowling? Mr Hornibrook I understand is their only slow left-hand bowler, and I am a slow left-hand bowler myself. I was elated to read of Mr J. C. White's success in Australia, and as soon as he came back I hurried to Lord's to see him. To my horror I discovered that he did not know what slow left-hand bowling is. I would have called it (and did so) fast left-hand bowling. You say nothing of bowling in *The Times* except that you were out first ball, so that perhaps you find all bowling alike and inclined to be fast. Now my left-hand bowling is so slow that it exasperates the batsman, who has gone through all his flourishes by the time the ball reaches the middle of the pitch. My bowling does not so much take the wickets as lie against them. If I think I have sent down a bad delivery I can pursue the ball, recapture it, and send it down again. Ought I to tell Mr Hornibrook about this, or would it be more patriotic to tell Mr White, or should they be left to go on in the old way?

Do you feel a special interest in the very young Australians? I do, especially in Master McCabe, who is so young that his schoolmaster has had to sign 34 rules not to appear on the field and take him back to school. There are also Mr Jackson and Mr Bradman. I know something that is going to happen to all three of them, besides centuries. At some period in a Test Match they will be found in a dressing-room, each one drooping on a seat and murmuring in anguish: 'Oh gosh, oh gosh, why did I play forward to that ball!' Ought I to prepare them for this, or leave them looking happy with 97 on the board?

Perhaps wisest to give them no tips. A side that can leave out Macartney needs them not or is mad. Did you ever see a swallow with a sense of humour chased by dogs? It would come down close to them to tempt them, then soar, then down again and soar again, and so round and round the lawn. That was Macartney with his bowlers. They say Jackson is such another. How splendid! I mean, Oh, dear! Such a talk we shall have if you will dine with me.

J. M. Barrie

The next day, on Thursday 1 May, whole columns were devoted to such an interesting subject. Some correspondents read much between the lines.

CRICKETERS ALL

'A Subtle Propagandist'

Sir, There is an appealing ingenuousness about Sir James Barrie's dinner invitation to the Brigadier that is most disarming. That is, at first reading. But it behoves us Australians to be wary at this time and to scrutinize closely anything that relates to cricket. A second reading somehow brought to my mind the stage *ingénue* and I began to associate her deadly demureness with the charming innocence of Sir James's invocation of the guest. Suddenly my worst suspicions were aroused. There was more than met the eye in Sir James Barrie's sympathetic leaning towards Australians in having, batting or fielding, to remember all the clauses in their touring contract; also well simulated was his solicitude for the very young Master McCabe and the not-quite-so young Mr Jackson and Mr Bradman in their dismay at playing forward to the ball that dismissed them. But was it genuine? One can but shake one's head over such guile and murmur, 'Ah! here indeed is a subtle propagandist!' And all under the guise of a hospitable impulse towards the Brigadier.

We all know that no game has any terrors for youth. While they confidently step out and hit, they could walk half-way down the pitch and greet with a cheer Sir James's slow-motion left-hand googly. And if it got by they could, on his own showing, step back and have another couple of cracks at it before it reached the wicket. He wants that ball to curl up like a serpent in the minds of our imaginative youngsters and to poison and generally disturb their whole cricketing metabolism. If Sir James Barrie publicly asks anyone to sup with him I now have little doubt it will be to convince Mr Bradman that he has a hole in his bat. In Australia we do our barracking orally, from the seats round the oval. As to the famous English batsman, who had hit only three fourers from five balls, 'Come on, old man, make it snappy; you're disappointing us!' It is quite obvious that Mr Kelly will have to draft yet another clause for the young Australians' contract. It is not water-tight, for the Australian Board of Control could not foresee this kind of thing. The clause might read:

> Whereas it has come to our notice that subtle propaganda calculated to induce nervous anxiety is being issued to undermine the match temperament know ye by these presents that no invitations direct or indirect to yourselves or others to accept hospitality may be read by any member of the team.

It would seem that the Australian High Commissioner was 'getting hot' when at the reception at Australia House he warned our cricketers to beware of hospitality.

Yours faithfully,
Claude McKay

To the Editor of *The Times*
Sir, Sir James Barrie makes use of your columns to invite the Brigadier to a *tête-à-tête* dinner. Is this fair? Is this playing the game? We should all like to ask the Brigadier to dinner.

As a humble member of the Royal Literary Fund team, may I suggest that Sir James Barrie, who is to preside on his seventieth birthday at the one hundred and fortieth birthday dinner of the Royal Literary Fund, should invite the Brigadier to dine with us all on that occasion at King Edward VII Rooms. Then all who attend the dinner would have an opportunity at least of seeing one who has written himself so wise, so dauntless, and so human.

Yours truly,

James H. Blackwood

The *Times* own correspondent, having given a lengthy résumé of the story thus far, drew his own conclusions. 'Is it possible that Barrie wrote "The Brigadier's Exit" in order that he might have the satisfaction next day of writing his letter to *The Times*? Perish the thought.'

THE SPOKEN WORDS

'THERE is no surer sign of mediocrity than being accepted as a successful after-dinner speaker.' If Barrie did not actually eat his own words they surely found an exit soon after the dessert.

It was not really until the 1920s that he found the confidence to fully accept this new role, after his memorable oration on 'Courage' at St Andrew's. His legendary shyness, which had permitted captivating conversation in the select company of friends, did not readily allow such emissions in a public forum. And, of course, he could test the definition of friendship to the full, 'as some one you can be silent with'. But not, of course, in front of a strange audience, where there was no respite.

E. V. Lucas thought Barrie the most amusing after-dinner speaker he had heard. 'He leaves nothing to chance, both preparing and committing to memory; yet conveying the impression of weary improvisation. He also prefers a butt, or several, whom he finds in the room. I should not, however, call him a good talker. In fact, as often as not, he is the reverse: a discourager of talk in others, an absolute non-conductor. But whatever he does say – and he is often more vocal with new acquaintants than with old – is good, wise, humorous and, not infrequently, sardonic.' A guest at one dinner likened him to, 'Peter Pan at the speaker's wicket, making big hits off every ball.'

Barrie was an actor. He knew how to bewitch. The burr of his native parts was no hindrance. He instinctively judged the length of a pause and the pitch to adopt. 'And, although he meant all that he said, he meant also a great deal more than he said.'

At a prize-giving at Dumfries Academy on 30 June 1893:

I was glad to hear what Mr Chapman said about this magnificent idea of building a new school in its own grounds, with play fields all round. When that time comes, I used to think when I was a boy – in fact I used to think a great deal more of it then than I do now – that prizes should be presented to those who make the best averages at cricket, who kick the best ball at football and so on. There were no prizes given for that in those days. I don't know whether there are now or not. In those days we used to do our best without the help of the people with thousands, those shabby people with thousands. What we used to do was this. We used to write to every boy, to every man who had been a boy at Dumfries Academy, who had a cousin who had been at Dumfries Academy – who had been at the Station – or anything like that, to give a subscription to our cricket and football clubs. It seems to me that's about the most vivid recollection I have. We used always to be writing for subscriptions to cricket and football clubs. Now, since I left the Academy, no boy has ever written to me for a subscription to a football or cricket club. That's amazing. I'm sure you're much better behaved than we were. You behave much better today than we did. But in this, you're below us. It's your duty to write to all old boys and get subscriptions. I'm sure any of us who came back and found you had neglected your duty in that respect would tell you were almost – duffers.

For his speech at University College, Dundee on 5 May 1922, Barrie allowed himself considerable artistic licence with regard to his anecdotes. It was a common practice with him. Fact and fantasy had become so interwoven that it could only have been with the utmost difficulty that he could remember the difference. Impudent expositions of his own feelings after scoring an incredible and imaginary century, or pat punchlines such as 'our adversaries had once made 14, but we nearly won' were mixed with actual events like the occasion when notching a notable victory over the Artists having just been given a bat by C. B. Fry.

I agree with a great deal of, though, I regret to say, not with all the words that have fallen from your Chancellor. I agree at all events as to the necessity for having these athletic games. If I had to build a University, that would be one of the first things I would turn my attention to. I want to tell you for the last time – because I cannot get anyone to believe it – how extraordinarily good at football I was at

college. It is a solemn fact that I was seriously considered for the
Scottish fifteen. However, I will not go on with it; not a soul will
believe me. The Chancellor believes me – (*Earl Haig* – '*Everything
that Sir James says*') – with regard to cricket. Cricket is my game. I
was a great deal amused a few minutes ago when I sent down a few
pretended balls to Principal Irvine. I was put in an awkward position.
I did not want to get him out. I don't know whether you observed –
you did not seem to observe – that I bowled all the time to him with
my left hand.

I could tell you a little about my experiences in cricketing. I had a
literary team in London. For years I had thought of it. I had a great
knowledge of the game, except in the actual playing thereof. But I
used to walk about in Surrey, and with another man I used to watch
the villagers, and we used to think that we would play some of those
villagers when they got a bit older. We got to a decrepit old village
one year, and we challenged them. We set out with a team of
well-known people.

Going down in the train, I had to teach them the game. Though it
was only three-quarters of an hour, they were terribly full of confidence. One man always kept saying, 'Intellect tells in the end.'
They were such a terrible lot, and as we were discussing the name of
the team, I asked an African traveller – who was one of them, and
who had just come from Morocco – and who, by the way, constantly
ran away at the end of each over and had to be brought back for
another – I asked him what was the Moorish for 'Heaven help us'. He
said, 'Allah Akbar', and we first called ourselves that, but eventually,
in compliment to me, the name was turned into the 'Allahakbarries'.

Well, we got down to this field, and all seemed well. I told them
what would happen when somebody called 'Over'. I won the toss,
which I think all good captains ought to do. And I sent the other men
in, to teach my side the game. They had a nasty fellow, an innkeeper
– a left-handed innkeeper – who hit very hard. And after a bit I left off
bowling myself and put on various men to bowl. One man was so
terrible once he started we could not get his over to a close – there
were so many – what do you call them? – 'No-balls'. At last our turn
came. I sent my team in, and I put in first the man who said intellect
told in the end. He went in quite confident, and we all held our

breath, and there was a mighty whack, and we all cheered and we saw him come out. He was caught by the local curate at point. I soon had to go in myself to stop the rot. While I was batting, and knocking them about a bit – we made 11 altogether – a man of a rare scholastic turn came in, and he indicated that he wanted to say something important. I went and met him half-way along the pitch. He said, 'Should I strike the ball to however small an extent I shall run with considerable velocity.' I don't think we went in again, but they went in again, and then that horrible innkeeper came forward, and the way we finished it was by saying to the innkeeper that we all wanted to come and dine at his inn. And so he went away and we got him out. We were a good deal elated by that first match of ours, and our spirits began to run very high.

We went down next year. There were only nine of us who turned up. We drove about looking for two men to complete the team. We found a soldier sitting outside a public-house drinking beer with two ladies. We asked him to come and play, and he said he would if we would take the ladies. We took the ladies, and this man made 72. The last we saw of him was sitting at another public-house with two other ladies. Our last experience was at Broadway, where Mary Anderson, the famous actress, lived. She challenged us. She was frightfully keen, but could not learn the game. She had a professional to teach her husband, who was champion lawn tennis player of New York, but was no good at cricket, which is a different thing. I wanted him to make some runs to please her, and I told my men to bowl wide – as I was bowling today – and if they got a catch to drop it somehow. But we could not get that man to make runs however wide we bowled. If you fumbled a catch it got into your pocket. She used to be very depressed about this. She did not know the game; she called it 'crickets'. I remember the other side had been in first, and then we went in, and, after a varied fortune, I was out and things were looking a little blue for us, but a few runs were made by some of our men and we passed their score. She continued to run round the course in a great state of excitement, and I said, 'Don't bother any more; we have passed the score already.' She said, 'Yes, but you have still several men to go in.'

Our last match, with which I conclude these tremendously long remarks, was played at Esher against a team of real cricketers. They had five 'Blues' playing, and they had not been beaten that year. They went in first, and we began to get them out like anything. They were twenty times better than we were, but somehow we had all the luck. They got terrified and sent to London by telephone for a famous county player, who arrived just in time to be bowled. They made 50 or 60, and then we went in. I sent a parson in first, who was a frightfully hard worker, but a good cricketer. He had not played for some time, and was off his head with excitement, because he was having a holiday. He sang all the time because he was in such a state of glee, and he further annoyed them by running up the wicket to meet the ball half-way. That man made 135. They were in a dreadful state about this. We never cared whether we won or lost. We played the game. I was sorry for them too, and let them go in a second time; and, in order to give them a chance, I went on to bowl at one end with my left hand, and put another writer, Mr A. E. W. Mason, on at the other. My better class of bowling is slow. Its whole cunning lies in this – it makes me laugh to read in the papers about people being slow bowlers – they don't know what slow bowling is. You go on flourishing and flourishing, preparing for the ball more and more widely, and when you finish, the ball is just about half-way down, but pursuing its relentless way to the wicket. Mason, on the other hand, is fast, but somewhat erratic. He may hit the wicket, but is as likely to hit square-leg in the stomach. We began to get their wickets, and after two or three fell, the great county man came in. I was bowling, and I was hoping he would make a big score. At my second or third ball, as soon as the ball left my hand, I said to myself, 'Good Heavens, he is done for.' There it went, on and on, and he took a mighty swipe at it, and then let it lay like an exhausted man against the wicket.

Ladies and gentlemen, thank you all.

Barrie spoke again that day at a luncheon in the banqueting room of the Caird Hall:

I have just come from the Athletic Club, where I sent down an over to Lord Haig, which seemed to make him very uncomfortable. I could

[161]

not help recalling the day when Kirriemuir and Dundee were great antagonists at cricket. I expect they are so still. They are great opponents, friendly opponents, in everything. As to which is the greater town, I do not know. But so far as cricket is concerned, I remember the old matches on the Hill of Kirriemuir; and, so far as I can recall, Kirriemuir always won. I only played twice in these matches myself. The first time I made 1; but the second time I was not so fortunate. Well, ladies and gentlemen, I want to finish with some good words. I will finish with wishing good fortune and every prosperity to St Andrews and Dundee. They are good words for me to say. Good-bye to all; and I pass for ever, as I now do, out of public life.

Fortunately, he did not. Two years later, Barrie received the freedom of Dumfries and, at a dinner given at the Royal Restaurant, finished his homily to his old school friends with the following words:

Well, on the understanding you are all going to follow my example, I will tell you what was the great moment of my life. Unfortunately it happened only in the summer of this year, when I was asked by a cricket eleven of undergraduates playing against a Gloucester village team – the county of the Graces, remember – to fill a temporary vacancy – and they put me on to bowl, and I did the hat trick.

Barrie's speech to the Australian Cricket Eleven on the occasion of the luncheon given by the London District of the Institute of Journalists on 20 April 1926 was reproduced in the pages of *The Times*. Clement Shorter had the idea of circulating a limited edition among his friends and, after Barrie had corrected the proofs, twenty-five copies were printed.

How much sweeter those sounds (*of loud cheers for the speaker*) would be to me if I had got them for lifting Mr Mailey over the ropes. If I were to say one-tenth of what I could say about cricket, especially about my own prowess at it, there would be no more play to-day. Once more I buckle on my pads. I stride to the wicket. I take a look round to see how Mr Collins has set his field – and, oh horrible! I see

Mr Gregory waiting in the slips. What can he be waiting for? I get one consolation from Mr Gregory's name – he is obviously a MacGregor. I have no doubt that he inherited his bowling from his ancestor, Rob Roy MacGregor, who, as the books tell us, used to hurl rocks at the stumps of the Sassenach. Mr Gregory is now joined in the slips by Mr Hendry and Mr Mailey. Three to one! I don't know what they think they look like, with their arms stretched out imploringly, but to me they look as if they were proposing simultaneously to the same lady. Even though one of them wins her, what can he do with her? I hope they will remember this in the first Test Match, and that it will put them off their game.

The first Test Match! Fancy speaking that awful mouthful in words of one syllable. All the awful words this year are to be in one syllable. The three T's – Test, Toss, Tail. The first Test Match is about to begin. We are all at Trent Bridge. The English captain wins the toss – and puts the Australians in. I think he must have something up his sleeve. I don't quite catch sight of his face, but I saw him having a secret conversation with Mr Warner's old Harlequin cap, and I believe they are up to something. Maurice Tate takes the ball. You know his way. He then puts his hand behind his back; an awful silence spreads over the universe. The Prime Minister, in the House of Commons, in the middle of his speech is bereft of words. It has been said, probably by Mr Gregory, that drowning men clutch at straws. On a balcony in the pavilion nine members of the Australian team pick up straws and clutch at them. Mr Noble pauses in the middle of drawing up the complete Australian averages of the tour. Mr Hill in Australia is suspended between Heaven and the inkpot. Maurice Tate takes a little walk, which is to be followed by a little run.

My lords and gentlemen, pray silence while Maurice Tate delivers his first ball. There is now nothing to be heard except Mr Gregory letting fall his straw. Tate comes rushing forward and sends down, not the ball, but the seam. What does that mighty roar from the onlookers mean? Have the Australians already made four, or does it mean, in journalistic phrase, 'The next man in is Macartney'? Much good that will do us! Then there is Ponsford, who, I am told, has only been out twice in the last five years.

[163]

I suppose I am the only man in the room who knows what is to be the constitution of the English XI. Mr Warner and his committee don't know – at least I haven't told them. On such an occasion as this it may seem a little cruel to damp Mr Collins, but I suppose the truth is best, and I am afraid I must tell him that this year there is no hope for his gallant but unfortunate company. Our team is mostly new, and is at present hidden away in cellars. Our fast bowler – I mention this in confidence – is W. K. Thunder, who has never been known to smile except when he hears Mr Gregory referred to as a *fast* bowler. Of our batsmen, I shall merely indicate their quality by saying that Hobbs is to be 12th man. Of course, things *may* go wrong. There is the glorious uncertainty of cricket. But even though Australia should win – this time – I have a rod in reserve for Mr Collins. In that case I shall myself choose the Scottish XI. My first choice is MacGregor, with him Macdonald, Macaulay, and Macartney. Two other names as Scotch as peat are Hendry and Andrews. A. W. Carr is my captain, M. D. Lyon my wicket-keeper, and there are still Douglas, Nigel Haig, MacBryan, and Armstrong. With this Scottish XI. I challenge the Australians. The game not to be played on turf or matting, but as always, on our native heather.

In conclusion – for I was out long ago (caught Gregory) – in conclusion, as Mr Grimmett said when he went on to bowl in the last Test Match – let us pay our opponents this compliment, we are sure that if we had not thought of cricket first, they would have done it, and whether we win or lose, O friendly enemy, you cannot deprive us of our proudest sporting boast, that it was we who invented both cricket and the Australians. And let us not forget, especially at this time, that the great glory of cricket does not lie in Test Matches, nor county championships, nor Sheffield Shields, but rather on village greens, the cradle of cricket. The Tests are but the fevers of the game. As the years roll on they become of small account, something else soon takes their place, the very word may be forgotten; but long, long afterwards, I think, your far-off progeny will still of summer afternoons hear the crack of the bat, and the local champion calling for his ale on the same old bumpy wickets. It has been said of the unseen army of the dead, on their everlasting march, that when they are passing a rural cricket ground the Englishman falls out of the ranks for a moment to look over the gate and smile. The Englishman, yes, and the Australian. How terrible if those two had to rejoin their comrades feeling that we were no longer playing the game! I think that is about the last blunder we shall make. I ask you to drink to the glorious toast of cricket, coupled with the name of one of the greatest of all cricketers and one of the greatest of cricket captains, Mr Warner.

The speech was a huge success, interspersed with uproarious laughter and ending to 'thunderous' applause. A year later, *The Times* was again present to record Barrie's talk entitled 'Captain Hook at Eton', which was delivered to the First Hundred at Eton College on the eve of the annual encounter with Harrow at Lord's, though strangely enough there were no allusions to cricket.

In 1929, at the opening of the Glasgow Health Exhibition in the Kelvin Hall, Barrie had the chance to turn the clock back sixty years:

I am an old Glasgow Academy boy. I was only eight or nine at the time. Today, since my arrival in Glasgow, I have met a man who was with me there, a well-known man to you, a well-known Lord Provost here, Sir Archibald M'Innes Shaw. He thought I had forgotten all about it; it was so long ago. I said to him, 'Dr Morrison was the Rector,' and he said, 'Yes, and Marr was the teacher.' I corrected him and said, 'Billy Marr.' Then he said, 'The French master was Amours.' And I said, 'The German master was Scholack.' And so we went on. At that time I was living in Burnbank Terrace, near the cricket ground of Glasgow Academicals – probably it is not there now. And I used to be allowed to throw up the balls to the fielders, and I dare say he used to be allowed to do it too. And if my five minutes had been ten minutes, I dare say I could have remembered how they sometimes let me bat for a little against his bowling, and I hit it all over the field.

In June 1930, the Allahakbarries (in name, at least) made positively their last appearance. Barrie was being awarded the freedom of his home town, Kirriemuir, and presented the cricket club with a new pavilion, which still stands to this day and houses one of the few camera obscuras to be found in the country. His speech in front of a large crowd at the cricket ground was full of reminiscence:

The first school I was at was Howie's, but I was only there for one day. Ran away. The Prime Minister [Ramsay MacDonald] has told me that he was under Howie for years – in some little place farther north. Strange to think that if I had stuck to Howie and he had run from him, he might today be twelfth man in the Allahakbarries and I might be flying in an aeroplane to Lossiemouth.

The cricket match was between the Allahakbarrie team – for which the Australians Macartney and Mailey were to appear; Barrie was taking no chances, after all, he was twelfth man – and the West of Scotland.

I must not delay you further, for the cricketers are avid to begin, and we to watch them. I think we are very beholden to our distinguished architect and to those who have helped him to carry out so success-fully my idea of a whistle. And to the West of Scotland for so boldly challenging us. And to the famous Australian cricketers who now become Kirriemarians. Our site on the Hill is as grand as Broad Ha'penny, the cradle of cricket, and the outlook is one of the fairest in our land. May doughty deeds be done here with bat and ball and at the goal-posts.

My love for cricket began as I sat on the Hill cheering for renowned Kirrie Club. I see them still, pausing at Charlie Wilkie's lodge to pick up their implements, sometimes even letting me help to carry the cricket bag. The bats, I believe, were made by Jock Wright the joiner. Peter Lindsay was after my time, and, alas, I never saw him smite them. But I remember some of the players; yes, and their action at the crease lingers like music in my mind. Dundas with his wily underhands, Morrison our stylist, Doig whom we welcome back today, Haggert, Stewart, Worlie who was always out trying to make a six, Alec Lowson. It is good to know that Mr Lowson is with us still. May he often sit here and recall, as I do, how he used to mow the wickets down. Ladies and gentlemen I now declare the pavilion open for play.

The *Kirriemuir Free Press* reported the match fully:

Sir James Barrie went out with the two captains, Mr David McGregor, Kirriemuir, and Mr K. I. D. Mathieson, West of Scotland. Sir James spun the coin and the Glasgow side won first lease of the wicket.

J. A. Dunnet and Rev. A. G. Seymour opened the batting against the bowling of J. R. McGregor and D. Stevenson.

Dunnet made a splendid stand, and although he was not top scorer for his side was about the most useful bat in his team until he was unfortunately run out.

The West put on a score of 120, K. I. D. Mathieson, the captain, having the honour of winning the bat presented to the highest scorer with 30.

When Macartney and Mailey got together the batsmen were uncomfortable, and the bowling of this pair was a treat to watch.

Mailey was making the ball spin, and the batsmen were kept on tenterhooks. He had two wickets for 45.

Macartney, a swift bowler, had the splendid analysis of 6 wickets for 29 runs.

The local bowlers made a good impression. J. R. M'Gregor had 1 for 13; D. Stevenson 0 for 2; and J. Smart 0 for 7.

The Allahakbarries compiled a score of 168 for 4 wickets, winning the match by 6 wickets and 38 runs.

C. G. Macartney gave a stylish display with the bat, hitting freely all round and only once gave a hard chance. The West of Scotland captain kept shifting his field in an endeavour to get him out, but the famous Australian noted the changes and made his strokes through the gaps left. He compiled a score of 101 not out. On reaching his century he received a great ovation, and stumps were then drawn.

Mailey, the other Australian, did not get a chance to show his skill with the bat.

Scores:

WEST OF SCOTLAND

J. A. Dunnet, run out	18
Rev. A. G. Seymour, c Kettles, b M'Gregor	7
J. S. Milne, c Mailey, b Macartney	5
N. R. Bruce, c M'Lean, b do	5
K. I. Mathieson, c M'Gregor, b do	30
J. Wilkie, b do	0
D. C. Daly, b Gerrand	0
F. Stead, b Mailey	19
G. E. Pole, c Smart, b Macartney	2
J. Pearson, b Mailey	9
J. C. Nicholson, not out	0
Extras	25
Total	120

ALLAHAKBARRIES

Major Garthwaite, b Wilkie	7
C. G. Macartney, not out	101
H. M'Donald, b Pole	19
W. C. Gerrand, run out	11
J. R. M'Gregor, st Nicholson, b Stead	9
D. M'Lean, not out	7
A. A. Mailey, G. Kettles, D. M'Gregor (capt.), D. Stevenson and J. Smart did not bat.	
Extras	4
Total for 4 wickets	158

At the conclusion of the game Mr Alex. Lowson was presented with the autographed bat with which the Australian played.

Mr Lowson, who met the Australians on behalf of Sir J. M. Barrie when they arrived at Forfar, was presented with a photograph signed: 'Alex Lowson, of the Allahakbarries, from his captain, J. M. Barrie'.

After the match the teams dined together, and Provost Peacock and Mr David Smith, Town Clerk, were present at this happy function.

One wonders what the Kirriefolk really thought of all this pomp. Their predecessors had always been suspicious of the little man, convinced that in his writings he was mocking them. How did he have such a reputation in London? How did he make money out of books? Conan Doyle, after a visit in the early days to the Barrie homestead, observed drily: 'Some people here think that Barrie's fame is due to the excellence of his handwriting. Others think that he prints the books himself and hawks them round London. When he goes for a walk they stalk him, and watch him from behind trees to find out how he does it.'

Whatever their private thoughts, the Kirriemurians showed no reservations in their welcome and it was a day of great nostalgia for many besides Barrie.

There was no doubt of Barrie's popularity with the Australians. For the tourists he seemed to have been assigned the position of chief speechmaker, for at a dinner given by the President of the MCC, Sir Kynaston Studd, in London on 8 September 1930, his services were once more in demand.

Sir Kynaston Studd said to me, 'If you know nothing about the game it does not matter. We must have a left-handed speaker.' I gathered from him that, in proposing the toast of the Australian cricketers, the first question to arise is how to get Woodfull out. Mr Woodfull is to reply to this toast. As I have something to say to him, I am very glad that he is not sitting near me.

Sir Kynaston said to me, with a tear in his eye, 'I suppose you may as well begin by saying that the better team has won,' but I saw that, in the doleful situation which we have really met, what was really needed was something more left-handed than that. It has struck me that Mr Woodfull might have prepared a few remarks on the assumption that I was going to say the better team had won. Therefore I have no intention of saying that the better side won.

[169]

Personally, between you and me, I have not the slightest doubt that the better side won. I would go further, I would say that I look upon this team as one of the greatest Australian teams. But Mr Woodfull, where are you? Don't you even think that I would ever admit it. The score board now reads o—1—o.

The next man in is——. Sir Kynaston made out a list of the various combatants, and he told me that when I mentioned this name it would be received with hearty but hollow cheers. The name, so far as I can make it out, is Mr Badman. I feel very sorry for Mr Badman. I do not doubt that he meant to do better. When the Australian team returns home they will be met, as we can well imagine, by countless thousands of Australians all straining at the leash to hear from Mr Woodfull which side won the Test Match, and when they hear there will be tremendous rejoicings. The team will be taken to hotels and public places and feasted, all with the exception of Mr Badman; he has carried this plan of his of not knowing how to get out to such an extent that he now cannot get out of anything. He won't be even able to get out of the ship when all the others are merry and bright. We now leave him pacing the deck, a dark and gloomy figure.

I warn you – Kippax, Ponsford, Jackson – I warn you all, if you go on as you are doing you will soon be in the same plight.

Down at the foot of the table there is a small boy – Mr McCabe. I don't know whether as a treat Mr McCabe will be allowed to attend banquets with the men. The nicest thing I have heard about the Australians is that Mr Ponsford and Mr a'Beckett used to sit up every night with Mr McCabe until he fell asleep because he was afraid of the dark. I know a boy who is a collector of autographs, and who has followed the Australian team to every hotel they have stayed at in England collecting McCabe's night-lights.

Mr Oldfield is smiling as if I was not going to say anything about him. The lovely way in which he pulls off those little things on top of the wicket without a sound! So courteous! You feel that, in the English way, he is saying 'So sorry.' What do you think would happen to Mr Oldfield if some day, when he was batting, he turned round and saw he was also keeping wicket?

I was told of Mr Wall that the day he was born his people had to call from the window telling him to lay down that ball and come inside. I should say from what I have seen of Mr Wall, that its only effect upon him was to make him take a longer run.

Sir James also referred humorously to other members of the team, adding, 'I think that is all of you. I just wanted to run through the side.'

In 1932, Barrie opened the Edinburgh Health Exhibition in the Waverley Market, Edinburgh. During the First World War, he had instituted a hospital near Verdun in France for children maimed amidst the combat.

They were really dreadfully sharp little children. They did things none of your children would have done. When they were playing, and nurses were in the offing with their thermometers, these children used to stop and hold their breath so that their temperature should not go up. I also taught them cricket with a ball of lint taken from the surgery, purloined from it, and with a bat that had been a crutch. I was sort of thinking now that it was I who purloined that lint. They had a very artful way of trying to get me to come out to play with them very early in the morning. They learned a few Scots words, taught them by a nurse who did not know the language, words like 'Reeky-reeky', 'Tam Shanter', and 'pot-ae-toes', which they thought so very Scots. They did not tell me about that, but they gathered under my bedroom window in the early morning and all shouted out those words to lure me down, usually quite effectively. They had a name for me. They called me 'Monsieur Auld Reekie'.

Yet again, in May 1934, Barrie addressed the Australian visitors. It was to be his penultimate public speech:

How can I, a Scot, dare to talk about the game in this den of cricketers? No Scot really knows anything about cricket.

You English and your games! It is many years agone since I left my kilted fastness and came to reside among you queer ones. Yet in a sense your cricket has got me. I too have fallen, O Lucifer! A month or more ago I thrilled – an English thrill – when I read in the newspapers – the Stop Press column – that the very day Mr McCabe arrived in London he went out for a walk. Gentlemen, that is what I did also the day I arrived. No one recorded it, but I now feel that I can say 'McCabe and I.' I hope he will make another 187 in a Test Match this year, and if he does I shall feel that I have a mysterious share in it.

I come out strong nowadays in argument about slow batting and brighter cricket. My proposition is that batsmen should follow the example of chess players in Spain, where chess contests are so long drawn out that combatants leave the continuance of the game to the second son in their wills. Again, I am permitted by Mr Leveson-Gower to announce that there is to be a Test Match soon at Nottingham, and I am of opinion that, if in this match Mr Bradman or Mr Ponsford is out first ball, it would be a sportsmanlike thing on our part to let him claim, as in our boyhood days, that he thought it was a trial ball.

Gentlemen, I admit I feel a drawing towards the Australians, and if I may say so, especially to their captain, but some of them are visiting these shores for the first time, and for their guidance while among you I should like to tell them how I first got to know the English. Soon after I reached London I was wandering in the pleasant lands of Surrey, near where the Tillingbourne runs, with an elderly Scottish clergyman, his first appearance in the South. By some fatality we paused at the window of the village shop, and therein was exhibited a placard which he read before I could hurry him away. We were a silent pair and we expressed our emotions without words.

I forget if I told you what was on the placard. It announced a local cricket match, Laity *v*. Clergy. I hope I don't need to tell you that in Scotland the clergy do not play games. We thought it our duty to proceed to the match. There another staggerer awaited us. The clergy were wearing white flannels! He had never conceived – neither had I – that they would be in anything but their blacks. In after years, though he and I talked of it privately, he never told them in the North about this strange affair, for the English had got round him, as they got round everybody except, perhaps, Grimmett, and he thought it would be shabby of him to let Scotland know. Perhaps it is shabby of me to let your Australians know. Indeed, how can I be sure that Mr

Wall and Mr Kippax and Mr Woodfull himself are not all reverend gentlemen?

Such are the English, but please do not believe, gentlemen, for a moment longer that Scotland does not love cricket, or that this Scot does not love it. I wooed it first in my little native town on the most delectable ground these eyes have seen; and I have been made happy of it for countless years at Lord's and the Oval, where you dwell among the great ones in the Pavilion while I represent low life among the mob. Sometimes as the years revolve I may get a little mixed between one year's games and another. I see now that the Australians here to-night are not perhaps the ones I had expected to find. Is Victor Trumper just a shade? The other day I was at Cambridge when the Australians were playing the University – no, it couldn't have been the other day, because I saw young Stanley Jackson there giving young Ranjitsinhji his Blue. A gay pair of boys they were. That moment at Fenner's journeys on with me like some unforgettable Biblical picture.

Has it ever struck you that cricket deeds and phraseology conjure up scenes as colourful as if we had them from the days of the prophets? When the day's play is over, Old Testament figures gather on the ground – Hobbs taking the first over while all the clocks have stopped; classic Oldfield diving while the policemen sob round the ropes – the gay Macartney comes down the steps – behold disdainful Woolley telling the ball to go away. We here to-night, gentlemen, share a lovely vision, we have all seen the hand of Chapman taking swallows on the wing.

Is cricket politics? Go to. May I venture, before I sit down, to say what I think cricket is? Cricket is an idea. It was an idea of the gods. They looked at poor humanity and its often tragic efforts, and though we made them wince we occasionally found favour in their eyes, and they sent us gifts – a little fortitude, a sense of fairness, an unconquerable gaiety of heart, and perhaps an aphorism about the wisdom of sometimes forgetting. They did not send those gifts to us one at a time, they rolled them up into quite a little ball and tossed it down to us. The name cricket is ours. Any genius could have invented it. But its meaning is theirs. The ball does not, as is generally supposed, contain ashes, it contains a living thing, a winged word about

[173]

'playing the game.' The immortals left it at that, for cricket is the only game they play themselves. If we don't continue to play it in that spirit, posterity may forgive us, but we shall be accurst of our forebears. You will find all about it, gentlemen, in the lost books of Homer.

It is a great pleasure to couple with the toast of the Australian cricketers the names of their captain and manager. They could not wish for a better manager. As for Mr Woodfull, we not only acclaim him, we thank Australia for him. Those gods would be here to-night to sing his praises were it not that they are already at Trent Bridge making sure of their seats. We rejoice that he brings with him many who have charmed us on a previous occasion. Bradman, when you were here before, we knew that another prodigy had arisen in the land of cricket; you won every garland batting can claim except one only, yours did not seem to issue sufficiently out of excess of joy and gaiety to win the love of greybeards, but the other day at Lord's you did enter into our love. We also welcome the new men. We welcome you, Mr O'Reilly and all, with affectionate disquietude. As for our kindly hosts of the Surrey C.C, how much better you would be employed, gentlemen, if instead of listening to me you would now go out into the highways and byways, and join in England's searching, searching, searching for eleven fast bowlers!

The bowlers are still to be found. Barrie had an entertaining habit throughout of his speeches of attributing all his apparently less worthy opinions to another sublimation, an *alter ego*, a fellow-friend, M'Connachie. It was a convenient form of what has been called interior monologue, though A. A. Thomson was perhaps more accurate in his description of the ruse as 'interior duologue'. In effect, it had similarities to a two-man comedy routine albeit, of course, from the one person. A sort of ventriloquist without the dummy.

Barrie's death in 1937 was rewarded by an abysmally inadequate four and a half line obituary in *Wisden* the following year. Nothing at all about the Allahakbarries, nothing about the inspiration and joy that he gave to thousands of cricketers and thousands more would-be cricketers in his plays, books and speeches, nothing about . . . But Barrie, we must remember, was not *Wisden* material. Fundamentally, he lies within the nooks and crannies of the game, on the ephemeral fringe, where all its inherent quirkinesses and queer happenings are cultivated for all the right reasons.

Among the relics of his life auctioned at Sotheby's five days before Christmas fifty years ago was a tattered copy of *The Boy's Own Book: a complete encyclopaedia of all the diversions* that had been given to Barrie by the widow of Thomas Hardy after her husband's death. Accompanying the book was a note: 'When T.H. was twelve years old he used to stare at this work in a bookseller's window at Dorchester and crave to have it as his own. He saved up his pence for this end. One night he went with his father and others as musicians to a wedding feast but was told to decline monetary reward. The revellers, however, dropped many pennies in his cap, and after an internal struggle he pocketed them and so (as he used to tell) was able to buy the book.'

For Barrie that book must have been a bible; after all, he had been diverted and diverting all his life. One hears faint echoes of a haunting and plaintive cry: 'The horror of my boyhood was that a time would come when I must give up games, and how it was to be done, I knew not . . .'

Barrie's everlasting triumph was that he never, never did.

APPENDIX I

LADIES AT CRICKET — THE ALLAHAKBARRIE CC

I lay beneath a cherry tree, the idle spectator of a cricket match between a ladies' school and eleven young women of the neighbourhood. Not long before, I had seen two teams of the softer sex scrimmaging over a football, hardly an edifying spectacle; but here they made a pretty picture, those happy girls, flitting and darting in print and flannel, and the field was vocal with them. The elevens wore at their waists a rose, a red rose for the school girls, for the others a Maréchal Niel; and the victorious side were to leave the field with the rose of the vanquished at their belts.

The captains tossed for first innings in a professional manner: but, owing to a little peculiarity in one of them, who could not toss the coin without throwing up the other arm also, the penny was lost and a postage stamp had to be used; it answered all requirements and was slow in coming down, thus adding to the suspense. Then the Maréchal Niels went to the wickets, of course padless, carrying their bats beneath their arms, while the tail of the 'out' side gathered round the crease to hem in the ball and have a little chat until it came their way. The first representatives of the yellow rose were Miss Rawlins and Miss Thoms, who both played at least as well as a junior boys' team and with fairly straight bats, Miss Thoms getting the first cheer for going out and patting the ground with her bat. The attack was entrusted to Miss Mitchell (swift daisy-cutters) and a tall girl familiarly addressed as 'Georgie' (overhand). The first over was a maiden, but off Georgie's second ball Miss Rawlins scored 1; following it up shortly afterwards by lifting Miss Mitchell heftily to the on for 2. The running between wickets was much faster than that of boys, once the bats-women started, but they lost time in watching the flight of the ball. Miss Thoms gave point a chance off a hard one, which was not taken, and then skied Georgie straight above short mid-on, who shouted 'Mary dear.' I found that 'Mary dear,' at present cover point, was their great catcher, and that wherever the ball was lofted the fieldswomen usually shouted for her. Several singles and a bye followed, and then Miss Mitchell found her way to Miss Rawlins's wicket (one for 11).

The next comer was Miss Philips, who immediately opened out to a tempting one from Georgie, and put her away to leg for 3. For this only 2 should have been scored; but long leg, instead of returning the ball, ran smartly with it to the stumps and put it personally into the wicket-keeper's hands. Miss Philips was now in superb form, and subjected the fielders to a rare piece of leather-hunting. Having driven Miss Mitchell for a brace, she cut another ball quite professionally, for which a couple was notched, and then running after a wide one, and overtaking it in the slips, hit it clandestinely for 3. This brought on Miss Coombes, *vice* Georgie; but runs still came, and the score stood at 25 after three-quarters of an hour's play. In stealing a run, however, the batswomen ran into each other, and before they could extricate themselves Miss Hibbert had told Miss Coombes what to do with the ball. (Two for 25.) Miss Epson, who came in second wicket down, did not seem at home with Miss Coombes, and, having slipped her in a fluky manner for 1, had her wickets spread-eagled. Thirty was brought on soon afterwards in byes, no long-stop apparently being securable who would do more than hasten alongside the ball. Miss Hibbert was substituted for Miss Mitchell, in the hope of getting another wicket before luncheon; but both batswomen played carefully, never hitting out except when they felt confident of raising the leather high in the air to some place where Mary dear was not fielding.

Play was resumed at 1.45, when the two not-outs (Miss Thoms, 7, and Mrs Tetch, 0) faced the bowling of Miss Hibbert and Miss Mitchell. Off the former's third ball Miss Thoms – who was now playing with more confidence – should have scored a pair; but Mrs Tetch, making a mistake as to her destination, rushed off in the direction of third man and was run out. (Four for 34.) Further disaster befell the 'in' side in the next over, Miss Thoms knocking off the bails with the skirt of her dress three times while turning to see whether Mary was fielding at long leg. She was then given out. Out she went in the jolliest way. They were all like that. Mary caught Miss Curson, and then the only altercation of the match arose, the Maréchal Niel captain coming out to complain that Mary was catching too many, and had no right to catch balls hit in the direction of another fielder. After consultation between the umpires the decision was given in Mary's favour. The two succeeding bats-women failed to score (also because of Mary). (Six, seven and eight for 35.) Mrs French, the next woman in, fell just as she was getting well set, and retired evidently under the impression that if you fall you are out. Things were now looking black for the Maréchal Niels, but the last wicket gave a deal of trouble, and a change of bowling had to be again resorted to. Miss Leslie drove, lifted, cut and spanked Miss Hibbert hard for 2, 1, 2 and 2, after which the end soon came, owing to Mary. It was charming to see the not-out player who had scored one lifting her cap to the pavilion and the red and yellow roses alike cheering her; but indeed throughout the match the teams played like white men.

The innings of the red rose was opened by Mary dear and Miss Wace, to the bowling of Mrs French and Miss Leslie. Mary took the first over from Miss Leslie, who has a dangerous delivery, pitching her balls so high that it is extremely difficult to reach them. Mary, however, has a leap that can reach anything, and 10 soon went up. The scoring now became fast and furious, Mary obtaining a complete mastery of the bowling and becoming so excited that she attempted once to catch herself.

With the score at 20, Mrs Tetch was tried at the pavilion end, but was only allowed to bowl one over, Mary hitting her so hard that it took five fielders to bring the ball back.

At 26 Miss Wace, whose shoe-lace had become undone, hit her wickets while retying it, and the next comer got a blob. With two of the best wickets down for 26, the prospects of the 'in' side were now less bright. Mary continued to smite them; but was at last dismissed by a cup of cocoa brought to her amid applause, or at any rate by the next ball, which fell into the hands of Miss Leslie, who found it there after looking for it on the ground. After a short interval for what was evidently the most delicious conversation, play was resumed. The result seemed a foregone conclusion with the score at 35 for three wickets; but a remarkable change came over the aspect of the game when Miss Curson was put on to bowl. In her first over she almost did the hat trick, her delivery being so swift that even the slips fled. With only four wickets to fall and 8 runs to get to win there was still a possibility of the Maréchal Niels pulling the match out of the fire, and the fielding now became so smart and clean that Miss Mitchell was thrown out by Mary, who had come on as substitute for a fielder. Bets in gloves were offered and taken by the two fieldswomen nearest me. By byes and singles the score rose slowly to 41, when Miss Mousey was cleverly run out, the stumps being knocked down at both ends. Miss Curson had now gone completely off her form, and Mrs French was again tried. At 42 Miss Croall would have been run out if Mrs Tetch had not paused to dust the ball before returning it. This lost the Maréchal Niels the match, for at 5.30 Miss Croall made the winning hit, a dashing blow into the deep, which was caught by Mary but not until the needed 1 had been run.

The gaiety of them was a new delight on cricket fields. The most successful bowlers were Miss Curson, who took three wickets for 7 runs, and Miss Leslie (three for 14). When all is said and done, however, the match was Mary dear's, who, I am incredibly informed, is a school-marm and the mother of two. I was also told that she cried on the way home because she thought she was such a rotten catcher. The distribution of the roses of the fallen among the victors was delightfully formal but ended in a gay race to the pavilion. As for myself, I continued to eat cherries; it seemed the right thing to do, in thankfulness for the lingering sun and for merry ladies.

APPENDIX II

There are two cricketing extracts in Barrie's work which deserve to be recorded:

a) In *Neil and Tintinnabulum*, in answer to his tutor's demand for a lengthy letter on one of three subjects, W.W.'s attempt on his favourite game reads, 'The game of cricket is my favourite game and it consists of six stumps, two bats and a ball.' He is then stuck and after wandering round the table many times he adds, 'Nor must we forget the bails.' (Stuck again).

b) In *Jane Annie*, Barrie's unsuccessful musical collaboration with Conan Doyle cobbled together on the beach at Aldeburgh, the last verse of the Proctor's song (played by Rutland Barrington) reflects both their passions:

> In an abstract way (though I don't care to play)
> I think very deeply of cricket
> And prove that because of dynamical laws
> It's easy to keep up one's wicket,
> I could score without doubt my hundred not out,
> Though modesty makes me refrain,
> And the whiz of a ball is not soothing at all
> To a man with a sensitive brain.
>
> His M.C.C.– ey
> And W.G. – ey
> Lords-and-the-Ovally brain.

APPENDIX III

When Barrie arrived by car at the new Athletic grounds at Fairmuir, Dundee, in 1922, he was 'chaired' by enthusiastic students to the cricket pitch where they had just finished an inter-College match. The local Advertiser took up the story: 'Parkes, the 'Varsity "prof" was standing with a cricket bat in his hand. McConnachie then took off his overcoat, and tying his scarf more tightly round his throat, he took the ball and induced Principal Irvine to stand at the wickets while he indulged in an over.

Principal Irvine: "Do you know that lunch is at one?"
Sir James: "I don't want any lunch" (laughter)

With his left hand, Sir James made six successive throws, which the Principal swiped amongst the crowd around the pitch, and the last was caught by a red-gowned youth, whose explanation of "Caught!" was re-echoed by Sir James and the game ceased.'

Earl Haig had now arrived and after fulsome speeches Barrie bowled a few balls at the new Chancellor whose batting style seemed hampered somewhat by his military attire. Colonel Freyburg then took a turn with the ball in the remaining few minutes of play.

BIBLIOGRAPHY

Dear Turley, ed. Eleanor Adlard. Frederick Muller, London, 1942.

Portrait of Barrie, Cynthia Asquith. James Barrie, London, 1954.

Allahakbarries C.C. 1893.

The Allahakbarrie Book of Broadway Cricket for 1899.

The Greenwood Hat, J. M. Barrie. Peter Davies, London, 50 copies printed privately 1930; first published 1937.

The Little White Bird, J. M. Barrie. Charles Scribner's Sons, New York, 1925.

M'Connachie and J.M.B., J. M. Barrie. Peter Davies, London, 1938.

When a Man's Single, J. M. Barrie. Hodder & Stoughton, London, 1888.

J. M. Barrie and the Lost Boys, Andrew Birkin. Constable, London, 1979.

Autobiography, Neville Cardus. Collins, London, 1947.

The Life of Sir Arthur Conan Doyle, John Dickson Carr. John Murray, London, 1949.

J. M. Barrie, W. A. Darlington. Blackie & Son, London, 1938.

J. M. Barrie, F. J. Harvey Darton. Nisbet, London, 1929.

Memories and Adventures, A. Conan Doyle. John Murray, London, 1924.

J. M. Barrie, Janet Dunbar. Collins, London, 1970.

The Young James Barrie, Michael Elder. Macdonald, London, 1968.

John Burns, Labour's Lost Leader, William Kent. Williams & Norgate, London, 1950.

Reading, Writing and Remembering, E. V. Lucas. Methuen, London, 1932.

The Story of J.M.B., Denis Mackail. Peter Davies, London, 1941.

Letters of J. M. Barrie, ed. Viola Meynell. Peter Davies, London, 1942.

Barrie, Thomas Moult. Jonathan Cape, London, 1928.

Bat and Ball, ed. Thomas Moult. Arthur Barker, London, 1935.

A Few More Memories, Mary Anderson de Navarro. Hutchinson, London, 1936.

Annals of Brechin Cricket, 1849–1927, Alfred O'Neill. Black & Johnston, Brechin, 1927.

The Definitive Edition of the Plays of J. M. Barrie, ed. A. E. Wilson. Hodder and Stoughton, London, 1928.

INDEX